# Opening the Mind and Generating a Good Heart

# Opening the Mind and Generating a Good Heart

The Buddhist Monk Tenzin Gyatso,
The Fourteenth Dalai Lama

Translated
by
Tsepak Rigzin &
Jeremy Russell

LIBRARY OF TIBETAN WORKS AND ARCHIVES

ISBN: 81-85102-44-9

Published by the library of Tibetan Works and Archives,
Dharamsala, H. P. (India) and printed at Indraprastha Press (CBT),
4 Bahadurshah Zafar Marg,, New Delhi 110002.

# CONTENTS

# FOREWORD

In keeping with LTWA's aim of publishing works which offer a broader understanding of Tibetan religion, history and culture, we have great pleasure in bringing out another book by His Holiness the Dalai Lama.

*Opening the Mind*, which was written in the early 1960s, presents a synopsis of the Buddha's teaching according to the literary tradition of the commentaries of the great Indian Buddhist masters, which formed the basis of education in Tibet's monastic universities. As such it is an example of the written tradition which has grown in Tibet from Indian roots to clarify and preserve the teachings received from the Buddha. The work concludes with a brief history of the development of Buddhism in Tibet.

*Generating a Good Heart*, originally given as a talk, is an example of how the oral tradition can apply the Buddha's teachings to the needs and circumstances of the listener. Drawing on the themes of Shantideva's *Guide to the Bodhisattva's Way of Life*, His Holiness gives an inspiring eulogy of kindness and unselfishness which culminates in the awakening mind.

The translators, both of whom were members of our Research and Translation Bureau at the time of translation, are to be commended for their straightforward translation of these works. Over the last two decades interest in Buddhism and His Holiness the Dalai Lama has grown considerably world-wide; we hope that this book will further nurture this interest and be of help to all beings.

Gyatso Tshering
Director, LTWA

Oct. 1995

# INTRODUCTION

Part One of this book, *Opening the Mind (legs.bshad.blo. gsar.mig.'byed)* is a work composed by H.H. the Dalai Lama in the early 1960s, in which he gives a survey of Buddhist teachings from the initial impetus to engage in practice up to the qualities of a consummate Buddha. While Tibetan Buddhism is generally thought of as a Mahayana tradition, this work shows that it is not exclusively so, for Tibetan Buddhism also incorporates the teachings and practices of the Hinayana, which are in fact the foundation of the Mahayana. Practitioners of both vehicles discuss the two levels of truth, whereby they ascend the five paths of their particular vehicle. On many occasions, His Holiness has emphasised the importance of seeking what is common between religions rather than their differences; here he explains a number of features common to all traditions of Buddhism as well as some points peculiar to Tibetan Buddhism.

Over the last two decades, as Tibetan Buddhism has become more accessible, readers may have become familiar with the Graded Paths of the Mind, or *Lamrim*, presentation of the Buddha's teachings which was developed in Tibet. The present work, however, belongs more to the Indian genre derived form the *Ornament for Clear Realisations* by Arya Maitreya, in which he synthesised and classified the main points of the Perfection of Wisdom Sutras. It is also notable that all the references cited here by His Holiness are to the works of great Indian masters. This is consonant with the Tibetan custom of consistently referring back to the original sources, that is, the tradition of Buddhism in India.

In giving an account of various aspects of Buddhist theory the work is very concise; this may lead readers previously unfamiliar with Buddhism to wish for further elaboration, which would traditionally be gained by consulting a teacher, while on the other hand providing others with a useful reference book. At the beginning, His Holiness states his intention of sharing the illuminating wisdom of the Buddha's teachings with those who do not otherwise have an opportunity of studying the great Indian treatises which form the basis of training in the great Tibetan monastic universities.These treatises are commentaries to the Buddha's teachings written by Indian masters concerning the five major topics of logic, the Perfection of Wisdom teachings, Madhyamaka philosophy, knowledge of the phenomenal world, and monastic discipline.The Perfection of Wisdom and the Madhyamaka philosophy are the core of these studies and the present work provides a synopsis of them for general readers. As such it is used as a textbook for the study of Buddhism in Tibetan High Schools in India.

Part One is concluded with a useful summary of the history of Buddhism in Tibet describing its early origin and later developments.

Part Two, *Generating a Good Heart,* is a translation of a talk given by His Holiness to a largely Tibetan audience in the principal temple, adjacent to his residence in Dharamsala, India, on March 19th, 1977. It consists of advice accompanying the simple ceremony of generating an awakening mind through prayer, which is often held at the conclusion of a course of teaching. The prayer used here—

> I go for refuge until enlightenment
> To the Buddha, Dharma and Supreme Community;
> By the virtue of my deeds such as giving
> May I attain Buddhahood in order to benefit wander-
> ing beings.

is one of the most common verses in Tibetan Buddhism.Either this or a similar verse is recited at the beginning of most rituals and religious practices to reaffirm the practitioner's motivation and commitment.The first two lines concerns taking refuge in the Buddha, Dharma and Supreme Community, which is the entrance into Buddhism in general, while the last two lines concern the awakening mind, the altruistic aspiration for enlightenment, generation of which is the entrance to the Mahayana.Thus the simple public ceremony of repeating this prayer together serves to reaffirm and revitalise the participants' fundamental Mahayana Buddhist motivation.Taking refuge is a response to realising the unsatisfactory nature of your own existence and the wish to overcome it and also entails a commitment to avoid harming others.Generating a good heart and an awakening mind is a response to realizing that all other beings are the same as yourself in wanting happiness and that you can but help them by attaining enlightenment yourself.

His Holiness' talk accompanying this simple but crucial ceremony draws largely upon the themes of Shantideva's *Guide to the Bodhisattva's Way of Life*. His practical down-to-earth advice on the virtues of reducing selfishness and generating a good heart towards others, helping them and avoiding doing them harm, is relevant to everyone whether he or she is Tibetan, Buddhist or not. The concern here is not so much with the technical aspects of developing the mind as with the manifest benefits of generating a good heart on a day-to-day basis, not towards some abstract goal, but towards the people and beings we live and associate with.

The juxtaposition of these two works *Opening the Mind* and *Generating a Good Heart* may be seen as revealing both introspective and participatory aspects of Buddhism, which are indeed means to fulfill the concerns of both self and others.

In accordance with His Holiness' intention of writing for those who do not have the opportunity for extensive study, we have tried to translate these works for a general reader. For this reason we have avoided a number of academic conventions such as the inclusion of Tibetan or Sanskrit equivalents of English terms within the text. We have presented the titles of other works cited in English only and have refrained from scattering the text with footnotes. However, we have prepared an explanatory glossary, a bibliography of works cited with their Tibetan and Sanskrit titles and a list of suggested books for further reading, which may be found at the end of the book. In translating *Generating a Good Heart* we have omitted His Holiness' preliminary remarks, which were addressed specifically to the Tibetans gathered before him at the time.

We would like to thank Geshe Sonam Rinchen for clarifying some difficult points in the Tibetan text; Kevin Garratt and John Newman for suggesting valuable improvements to the translation.

Tsepak Rigzin & Jeremy Russell
Dharamsala, February 1985.

# Part One

# Opening the Mind

# CHAPTER ONE

## *Reasons Why We Should Practise the Dharma*

Homage to the wisdom which fully reveals the omniscient mind.

At this point in the 5,000-year span of the teachings of the fourth Buddha of this era, we are approaching the time when the only practice of Dharma remaining will be observance of ethics. In the 20th century, the era of nuclear energy, tremendous progress has been made externally in the material sciences, while internally there remains a very great need for a corresponding development of the mind. According to Buddhist philosophy that is achieved through contemplation and meditation, therefore we need to understand how to practise them. In this book I shall explain these principally with a few plain words and comments to share this illuminating wisdom—which reveals the omniscient mind—with fortunate people who otherwise lack the opportunity to study the profound and extensive teachings of the great treatises.

All wandering beings equally desire happiness and do not want suffering, which is so not only for us intelligent humans, but also for the foolish and closed-minded, even down to the tiniest worms and insects. All desire happiness and wish not to experience even the slightest suffering. Therefore, both I and others must engage in the means which give rise to happiness and do not bring about suffering. For if we hope to find happiness by merely sitting and waiting and generating a strong wish, 'May I not find suffering,' we will be unable either to find happiness or dispel suffering. Therefore, we require an ability to implement the causes from which happiness arise and eliminate the basis that gives rise to suffering.

Whatever we may do, there is no more perfect and complete means of establishing the causes of benefit and happiness and the elimination of suffering and harm than practising the Dharma.

Relying on the Dharma we will be able to generate happiness and eliminate suffering in this life, the next life, and many future lifetimes. Taking this life as an instance, there is nothing superior to the Dharma in producing happiness and eliminating suffering; for example, there is a great difference between one who has understood the Dharma and one who has not, with reference to the degree of their mental and physical suffering and their ability to cope with them. If the importance of the Dharma is not understood and the benefits of the teachings are not integrated with the mind, when there is a strong feeling of sickness in the body, the mind cannot bear it; both body and mind are oppressed by great suffering and the agony of pain affords no opportunity to experience happiness. If the importance of the Dharma is understood, when the body experiences sickness, by seeing it as the result of previously accumulated wrong-doing, as being of the nature of cyclic existence and through wishing to take responsibility for the action by accepting the sickness, mental suffering will not be experienced. Consequently, external physical pain may be overcome by the inner power of mind, through which suffering will be dispelled. For that reason, mind is the principal factor controlling the body, while the body is something to be controlled. Thus, the mind's feelings of happiness or pain are the more powerful of the two.

Correspondingly, some people who wish to become rich through hoarding and guarding wealth, strive initially both mentally and physically, but experience the frustration of being unable to gather as much as they wish. In the process they experience the frustration of being robbed, losing their wealth or wasting it and being unable to protect it. Finally, whatever they do they must experience the suffering of being forever separated from their wealth, which passes into the possession of others. All these sufferings related to wealth and possessions are faults arising from not understanding the real meaning of the Dharma.

If we understand the teachings and see all riches as essenceless, like a dewdrop on a blade of grass, we will not experience the frustrations stemming from countless attempts to hoard and guard our wealth and from being unwillingly separated from it.

Similarly, when others insult, rebuke and speak unpleasant words to us, although an intolerable pain arises like a thorn at the heart, if we comprehend the teachings we can recognise their essenceless nature which resembles an echo. So, just as when an inanimate object is scolded, we will experience not the slightest mental turmoil.

Likewise, we suffer in this life from being unable to support our family and friends. We suffer personal defeat while others are successful, and so on. In brief, whatever physical or mental pain we have, such as gain and loss or happiness and misery, it is dependent upon wishes and anxiety. Similarly, fighting between nations creates destruction and fear and shatters innumerable people's happiness, of which only the name remains, while fomenting sufferings like a stormy sea. In short, any major or minor sufferings experienced in this life are the faults of either not understanding the Dharma or being aware of it but not putting it into practice.

If we practise the teachings we know, we will be able to stem the flow of all those sufferings. One might ask how this is possible; all such sufferings occur solely because of pride, miserliness and jealousy and the three delusions of attachment, aversion and ignorance, and so forth. Those faults of the mind are pacified and dispelled mainly due to the power of the Dharma, and contentment, a sense of shame, consideration and conscientiousness are adopted. Then body and mind enjoy nothing but peace, calm and happiness and unbearable pains do not arise. If we wish for joy and happiness in this life and do not seek suffering, it is important to understand the essential meaning of the Dharma and also to put it into practice.

To practise in such a way as to gain predominantly the happiness of this life is inadequate, because however great the happiness of this life, it is happiness that lasts only until death. However long life may be it will not last more than 100 years, and just so long will that happiness endure. Since the trail of future lives is long and hazardous, we need to give it some direction; thus we should strive for the means of finding happiness in and eliminating suffering from the stream of future lives. That too can be done only in conformity with the Dharma, never in accordance with other activities.

When it is explained that the goals of future lives must be accomplished, there are some who do not understand the Dharma, or who know a little but do not grasp the reasoning perfectly, who may think that the present mind depends simply on this body and that since past and future lives cannot be seen directly they do not exist. Such an opinion either maintains that if something exists it must be seen directly, or that the mind is produced in dependence on the body and that since the body is formed in dependence on the four elements, previous lives do not exist. It is thought that at the time of death the body reverts to the four principal elements, while the mind vanishes like a rainbow in the sky and that therefore future lives do not exist. Others, asserting that the mind is dependent on the body, consider that as the ability to intoxicate is an attribute of alcohol, so the mind is the attribute of the body. Others think that like the brightness of a lamp, the mind is a product of the body or that like a drawing on a wall the mind is a decoration of the body. Essentially, all these views assert that in this life it is not necessary for the mind which is produced at the time of birth to be generated from a corresponding mind, because it is born from inanimate elements. By way of example, it is likewise thought that intoxication resulting from drinking alcohol and the fire produced with a magnifying glass, etc., are results which arise from incongruent causes. Similarly, some dialecticians assert the non-existence of causality based on incorrect reasoning, stating that there is no agent creating the roundness of peas, the sharpness of thorns, nor the splendour of a peacock's tail, while it may be observed that the miser who never gives becomes rich, that killers live long, and so forth.

Moreover, others claim that some meditators absorbed in concentration have seen through clairvoyance that those who were miserly in former lives were subsequently born into rich families. For this reason they assert that although past and future lives exist, the principle of causality does not.

Yet others, when they achieve the concentration of formless absorption, mistake it for liberation. When they fall away from it and see that they must again take birth, they conclude that liberation does not exist.

Nevertheless, despite these various assertions, past and future lives certainly exist, for the following reasons: certain ways of thinking from last year, the year before that and even from childhood can be recollected now. This clearly establishes that there existed an awareness previous to the present continuity of awareness of an adult. Likewise, the first instant of consciousness of this life is not produced without cause, nor is it born from something permanent, neither is it produced from a solid, inanimate, incongruent substantial cause, therefore it must surely be produced from a congruent substantial cause. In what way are they congruent? Since a moment of mind is an awareness which is clear and knowing, it is preceded by a similar moment of mind which was clear and knowing. It is not feasible that such a preceding awareness be produced other than on the basis of a previous birth. Otherwise, if the physical body alone were the substantial cause of mind, then the absurd consequences of a dead body having a mind and a change in the body necessitating a change in consciousness would also ensue.

The substantial cause of mind is that which is suitable to be transformed into the nature of mind. Although the physical body may act as an auxiliary cause of subtle change in the mind, it is impossible for it to be a substantial cause. Something inanimate can never transform into mind, nor can mind transform into something inanimate. Although some may assert such transformations, justifying them with a few examples of changes in external objects, the way in which a non-physical mind changes and the way physical objects change are different. As an illustration, it is impossible for what is not space to transform into space, or for space itself to change into that whose nature is not space, and the changes in a non-physical mind are similar. Thus, with reference to the present physical body and non-physical mind, the substantial cause of the body is the blood and semen produced by the parents, but the parents' minds can never be the substantial cause of the present mind. For example, it is possible for a dull and foolish child to be born to intelligent parents, no matter how educated they are. From this it can be seen that there is no part of the parents' bodies or minds which transforms into their child's mind in this life.

Therefore, in reality the mind flowing from a previous life acts as the substantial cause of this mind and the blood and semen of our present parents act as the substantial cause of this body. As a relationship between the two was established by an action in former lives, a relationship exists between the mind and body of this life. Due to that, even a newborn baby or calf immediately after birth begins to eat or suck at the mother's breast without being taught. This is an indication of instincts left in the mind from previous lives.

As Acharya Maticitra says:

> The ability of the mind is unclear
> And the sense powers are dull by nature,
> Yet immediately after birth, taught by no one,
> We make efforts to eat food or
> Struggle to suck at the breast
> Through familiarity gained in other lives.

It is also unreasonable to think that past or future lives do not exist because they are not seen directly, for it is unacceptable to assert the non-existence of something merely because we have not seen it ourselves. We can understand this in this age of science and technology from our experience of seeing and hearing of many new external and internal discoveries, of which our forefathers in centuries past were unaware. Moreover, there are many who have seen past and future lives upon reaching a high level of concentration during intense meditation in reliance upon the Dharma. There are also many people who, because of previous instincts, recollect events from their former lives.

There are accounts of how, long ago in India, a Buddhist scholar debated with a Hedonist (Charvaka) and to prove the existence of past and future births directly to him, took the king and others as his witness, died and was reborn, later to become Acharya Chandragomin. Also in Tibet there were many who remembered their previous lives and on recognising people and objects from those times gave accounts of them.

Therefore, as future birth certainly exists for us, we must establish a definite purpose for it now. The way to do so is to strive in the means of becoming the embodiment of all good qualities and, through constant familiarity with a good heart, to exhaust all faults. Uninterrupted familiarity with the noble path in past and future lives, or reliance upon a profound method in this very lifetime, is the means to sever the continuity of cyclic existence, so the cycle of birth and death need be experienced no more.

# Chapter Two

## *Recognition of the Two Levels of Truth*

To begin with, we must understand how the two levels of truth are presented, how to practise the two paths of method and wisdom and how, dependent on them, the two resultant bodies are attained. Firstly, if we ask how the system of the two levels of truth is explained, *The Meeting of Father and Son Sutra* says:

> The knower of the world, without listening to others,
>     taught only these two truths,
> Whatever is conventional is likewise ultimate,
> There never exists a third truth.

Similarly, Nagarjuna's text *Root Wisdom* also says:

> Doctrines taught by the Buddhas
> Are perfectly founded on the two truths.

Objects of knowledge taken as the basic category can be divided into two classes, conventional and ultimate truths. When an object is directly perceived as being an ultimate truth, it ceases unequivocally to be a conventional truth. The same also applies to the perception of conventional truth and therefore the two truths are mutually exclusive. If either of the two truths did not exist, all objects of knowledge could not be classified within them, yet there is no third truth which is not one of these two. Thus the very mode of classification (into two truths) does not allow for the possibility of a third category.

The two truths are distinct; nevertheless, if they were not one in nature, four absurd consequences would occur: that a form's lack of true existence would not be that form's mode of being; that although form's lack of true existence is realised, that realisation does not overcome grasping at signs (of its true existence); that it would be meaningless for a yogi to meditate on higher paths; and, lastly, that even the Buddha has not burst the bonds of grasping at signs (of true existence) nor abandoned all the defilements which result in bad states of birth.

If the two truths were one and indistinguishable even in their isolates, these absurd consequences would ensue: as both actions and delusions, which are by nature conventional misconceptions, were eliminated, the ultimate reality of phenomena would similarly be eliminated; like conventional phenomena, ultimate reality would also have many different aspects; even ordinary people would perceive ultimate reality directly and, while remaining an ordinary person, one would abandon all obscurations and become fully enlightened. Therefore, the two truths are one in nature but distinct in their isolates.

Ultimate truth is the actual object found by a reasoning consciousness analysing ultimate reality. The mind which is involved with worldly terms and designations is called a conventional mind or a mind which is conventional, and the actual object found by it is a conventional truth.

In Sanskrit ultimate truth is called *paramartha satya; parama* means ultimate, excellent, etc., *artha* means purpose or meaning, *satya* means truth, permanent, etc. However, in this context, purpose does not denote the so-called purpose of self and others, but the object understood by an exalted wisdom awareness, the object of analysis, the object to be found. It is called ultimate because it is excellent, exalted and bears such significance. Unlike conventional fictions whose mode of appearance is incongruent with their mode of existence, its mode of appearance is congruent with its mode of existence, therefore it is called truth or ultimate truth. If ultimate truth is further categorised, Acharya Chandrakirti says in his *Supplement to (Nagarjuna's) Treatise on the Middle Way*:

> This selflessness was taught in two categories,
> That of persons and that of phenomena,
> In order to thoroughly liberate wandering beings.
> Therefore, the Teacher further taught
> Many aspects of it openly to the disciples;
> Thus elaborating, he taught 16 emptinesses
> And abbreviating them again taught four,
> Which are also accepted by the Mahayana.

So, both the selflessness of persons and the selflessness of phenomena may also be classified more elaborately as the four emptinesses which are: emptiness of functional objects, emptiness of functionless objects, emptiness of nature and emptiness of other entities; as the 16 emptinesses, internal emptiness etc.; as the 18 emptinesses; and as the 20 emptinesses. All extant phenomena which are not emptinesses are known as conventional truths. When those are classified more elaborately, it is stated in Vasubandhu's *Treasury of Knowledge*:

Heaps, doors of birth and classes are meant
By aggregates, sources and constituents.

There are five aggregates, 12 sources and 18 constituents.

### The Five Aggregates

| | |
|---|---|
| 1. Form: | This includes the five internal sense powers having form, eye sense power etc., and the five external objects, form, sound, smell, taste and tangible objects. These 10 with unrevealed forms make up the 11-fold form aggregate. |
| 2. Feelings: | The feelings of pleasure, pain and neutrality are the aggregate of feelings. |
| 3. Discriminations: | Conceptual and non-conceptual discriminations are the two components of the discrimination aggregate, each of which has three divisions—small, extensive and immeasurable. |
| 4. Compositional factors: | The aggregate of compositional factors includes both the collection of concomitant compositional factors, which include all the remaining secondary mental factors except feelings and discriminations, and the collection of non-concomitant compositional factors, which are neither form nor consciousness. |
| 5. Consciousness: | The aggregate of consciousness has six components, from eye consciousness to mental consciousness. |

## The Twelve Sources:

There are six internal sources: eye sense power, ear sense power, nose sense power, tongue sense power, body sense power and mind sense power. There are six external sources: form, sound, smell, taste, tangible object and phenomenon sources. Eye sense power and eye source are synonymous. Form aggregate and form are synonymous, yet form source and form are not the same, for a form source is only an object of eye consciousness such as colour and shape. Sound, sound source and object of ear consciousness are all synonymous and the same is true of smell, taste and tangible objects.

## The Eighteen Constituents

These are the six constituents of sense power which are supportive, eye etc.; the six constituents of consciousness, which are dependent, eye consciousness etc.; and the six constituents of observable objects, form, sound etc.

In short, all composite phenomena are included in the five aggregates, all objects of knowledge are included in the 12 sources as well as in the 18 constituents. Thus, all phenomena subsumed by the two truths are included in the 12 sources and the 18 constituents. If the constituents are further divided into detailed categories, there are 62. We should at least know the differences in their nature, function and classification and whether they are to be abandoned or not; thereby, we will come to master the six objects of knowledge, knowing which points are to be cultivated and which abandoned. In this way we will attain the bliss of liberation, forever freed from all sufferings.

# CHAPTER THREE

## *Reasons for the Presentation of the Buddha's Teaching as the Three Baskets*

It is because our mind and secondary minds are under the control of delusions that we continue to experience the spinning of the wheel of suffering in cyclic existence. If that is abandoned, liberation is attained; therefore we must principally subdue the delusions, such as attachment, in our mindstream. The Supramundane Victor, Buddha, taught the means to subdue them in 84,000 heaps of doctrine. If those are reduced, there are 12 scriptural categories. If condensed more concisely, they are known as the Three Baskets, which are the Basket of Discourses, the Basket of Discipline and the Basket of Knowledge. The reason for maintaining three baskets is stated by Arya Maitreya in his *Ornament for the Mahayana Sutras*:

> Nine reasons are accepted for the collections of teach-
> ings being condensed into two or three.

Of these nine reasons, three relate to what is to be abandoned, three relate to that in which to train and three relate to what is to be known.

First, the three objects to be abandoned are: the secondary delusion of doubt, the secondary delusion leading to the two extremes of conduct, and the secondary delusion asserting the superiority of one's own view. The antidotes to those are taught as the Basket of Discourses, the Basket of Discipline and the Basket of Knowledge respectively.

The Basket of Discourses clearly explains the aggregates, constituents, sources, dependent arising, the four noble truths, the grounds and the perfections, being primarily concerned with the training in meditative stabilisation. It dispels wavering doubts concerning the two extremes on the basis of the general and specific characteristics of phenomena. Therefore, the Basket of Discourses was taught as an antidote to the secondary delusion of doubt.

The Basket of Discipline prohibits engagement in all proscribed misdeeds such as sexual misconduct, attachment to external and internal sensual objects such as good food, clothes and dwellings which, when one is subsisting on alms, is an extreme of desire. However, if one maintains the immaculate ethics of renunciation, it is unnecessary to exert efforts to obtain wealth and so forth. When one has the ability to curtail strong attachment, one is permitted to make use of even luxurious clothes, food, dwellings and so forth. If one then imposes austerities upon oneself, it is an extreme. The Basket of Discipline was taught as an antidote to the secondary delusion leading to the two extremes of conduct, because it reveals the antidotes to both the extreme of austerity and the extreme of desire while subsisting on alms.

To summarise: if the delusions, attachment, pride, conceit and so on do not arise when one uses good food, clothes, dwellings, bedding etc., these are permitted by Buddha and a proscribed fault will not have been committed. However, if attachment etc. increases when using even meagre food, ragged clothes and the like, then a fault proscribed by the Buddha will have been committed. The principal concern of such permission and restriction is solely with the increase or decrease of the delusions, desire, attachment etc. within the mind, not with external objects.

The Basket of Knowledge clearly explains the specific characteristics of phenomena and their general characteristics such as impermanence, suffering and selflessness. Listening to, thinking about and acting on such teachings will automatically rectify the wrong views of purity, happiness, permanence and the conception of a self, from which spring the misconception that deviant ethics and ascetic practices are worthwhile. For this reason the Basket of Knowledge was explained as an antidote to clinging to the superiority of one's own view.

Next, the three reasons relating to that in which to train. The Basket of Discourses takes the three trainings as its subject matter, while the purpose of the Basket of Discipline is to establish the two trainings of ethics and meditative stabilisation, and the purpose of the Basket of Knowledge is to accomplish the training in wisdom. The Three Baskets were revealed in accordance with these three reasons too.

How do the three trainings of the Mahayana and Hinayana form the content of the Basket of Discourses? According to the ethics of the Hinayana, the Basket of Discourses explains the discipline of the individual emancipation vows which restrain the mindstream, the maintenance of completely pure behaviour and tradition, and the attitude fearful of even the slightest proscribed misdeed. It explains the concentrations of the states of mental stabilisation and formless absorptions, and the training in wisdom, which is special insight, seeing the four noble truths as they are.

According to the Mahayana, the Basket of Discourses explains ethics, such as restraint from misdeeds, the training in meditative stabilisations such as the 'Sky Treasure' and 'Going Like A Hero', and the training in wisdom, which is the non-conceptual intuitive wisdom that understands the ultimate mode of reality.

The Basket of Discipline describes the way to practise the two trainings of ethics and meditative stabilisation, for it shows unerringly what is to be cultivated and engaged in, and what is to be abandoned and refrained from. Thus, it specifically purifies ethics.

If ethics are pure in this way, we will not experience anguish or regret. Free from those, physical suppleness or ecstasy is attained and, dependent on that, mental joy and bliss increases. Consequently, the mind will not abide single-pointedly. Thus, the trainings in ethics and meditative stabilisation are accomplished by following the Basket of Discipline.

The Basket of Knowledge describes the way to accomplish the training in wisdom by clearly classifying the characteristics of all phenomena. Studying them generates the wisdom correctly cognising the characteristics of all phenomena, thereby specifically achieving the higher training in wisdom.

Lastly, the reasons relating to what is to be known. The Discourses explain the doctrine and its purpose, Discipline accomplishes the practice of the doctrine and its purpose, and Knowledge yields mastery of the doctrine, its purpose and related topics.

The Discourses reveal the inner meaning of the Dharma by explaining in great detail the terms, words and syllables and the meaning they convey, that is, the meaning of the aggregates, constituents and sources etc., or the aggregates and constituents etc., of phenomena; the meaning of the eight interpretive discourses or the doctrine of the path of 10 virtues by which to obtain high status, and the meaning of the 37 paths directed towards enlightenment, by which to gain the qualities of definite goodness. The purpose of this explanation is to enable one to train accordingly.

The way the Basket of Discipline achieves the purpose of the Dharma is that in leading to purity of ethics and through revealing the meditation on ugliness, the delusions are subdued. When such insights and realisations are actualised in the mindstream, the purpose of the Dharma is achieved.

Study of the Basket of Knowledge results in mastery of the doctrine, its purpose and related topics.

All the teachings of the Conqueror, which reveal the important points of the practices of method and wisdom of the three vehicles, as explained by these nine reasons, are contained in the Three Baskets.

When the whole content of the Three Baskets is condensed, it may be included directly or indirectly in the practices of the three higher trainings of ethics, meditative stabilisation and wisdom. Moreover, the ethics taught by Buddha are superior because they bring both direct and indirect benefits to self and others, whereas the teachings of the Forders and so forth, whose ethical and ascetic practices include self-mortification by means of five fires, are inferior because they bring pain directly and indirectly to self and others.

Likewise, the meditative stabilisation taught by Buddha is superior because it acts as an antidote to delusions and conceptual fabrications. Thus, it leads to happiness not only in this life but also in many other lifetimes, as well as the attainment of the bliss of liberation. The meditative stabilisation of the Heterodox avoids mental distraction to external objects and leads to happiness in this life. Yet no matter how good the fruit is, it can only lead to birth as a god of the form or formless realm. Not being an antidote to delusion or conceptual fabrications, it is inferior.

The wisdom revealed in the Buddha's teaching has the power to dispel the obscurations of grasping directly or indirectly at two kinds of self (i.e. of persons and phenomena), therefore it is superior. The wisdom taught by the Heterodox and so forth is incapable of severing the root of cyclic existence by revealing reality, therefore it is inferior. For these reasons, the ethics, meditative stabilisation and wisdom taught by Buddha are superior to others and are therefore called the three higher trainings.

# CHAPTER FOUR

## *Training in Ethics*

What, then, are the three trainings? First is the higher training in ethics which is the foundation of all qualities and a summary of the essential practices of Buddha's teachings. As Nagarjuna says in his *Friendly Letter*:

> Discipline is taught to be the foundation of all quali-
> ties,
> As the earth is for the animate and inanimate.

There are many kinds of ethics based on the discipline of avoiding the 10 unwholesome actions. When codified, there are three sets of these: the ethics of individual liberation, the ethics of a Bodhisattva and that of secret mantra.

As Acharya Vasubandhu says in his *Treasury of Knowledge*:

> Abbreviating them roughly,
> Ten paths of either virtuous
> Or unwholesome actions were taught.

### *Ten Unwholsome Actions:*

The 10 unwholesome actions are: three of the body—taking life, taking what is not given and sexual misconduct; four of speech—lying, divisive talk, harsh words and idle chatter; three of the mind—covetousness, malice and wrong view. These 10 paths of action are committed and accumulated through the three doors of the body, speech and mind.

### 1. TAKING LIFE:

There are five factors to taking life:

Object       — a sentient being of a different continuum from
                oneself.

| Thought | — | recognition (of the object). |
| Action | — | one's own act of killing or inciting others to kill, through poison, weapons or mantras etc. |
| Delusion | — | hatred in particular, and the delusions of desire, hatred and ignorance in general. |
| Completion | — | the victim dies before one does oneself. |

With these five the path of action of taking life is complete. If any of these factors are missing, the path of action will be incomplete, although a fault will still have been committed. This should also be understood with reference to the actions described below.

There are three categories of taking life: taking life through attachment because of craving for meat; taking life through hatred because of malice; and taking life through ignorance, as for example in making animal sacrifices. Of all the acts of taking life, taking that of a Foe Destroyer, one's guru or parents, ordained beings, the learned and so forth are the worst.

## 2. Taking What is Not Given

| Object | — | something owned by another or objects dedicated to the Three Jewels. |
| Thought | — | the wish to take something by stealth, force or deception. |
| Action | — | to take it oneself or cause others to do so. |
| Delusion | — | attachment in particular and the three poisons in general. |
| Completion | — | thinking that one has gained possession of the object, whether one has removed it or not. |

There are three categories of taking what is not given: stealing by force, such as robbing an innocent man; taking by stealth, such as breaking into a house; taking what is not given through deception, such as the use of false weights and measures. Of the acts of taking what is not given, stealing objects offered to the Three Jewels is the worst.

## 3. Sexual misconduct

| Object | — | a person in the care of others, a relative within seven generations, an observer of ethical discipline, such as a monk or nun, who are all |

improper partners. Even one's own spouse is an improper partner before images of the objects of refuge and so forth, and excepting the door to the womb other orifices are improper. Religious observance days, restoration and purification days, during pregnancy or menstruation and in the daytime are improper occasions.

Thought — the desire to enter (into intercourse).

Action — to do so.

Delusion — longing desire in particular and the three poisons in general.

Completion— the craving and gaining of the experience of orgasm produced by contact between the two organs.

There are three kinds of sexual misconduct: sexual intercourse with blood relations such as one's mother or sister; with those under protection such as another's wife; and those bound by religious precepts such as a monk or nun. Of the varieties of sexual misconduct, intercourse with one's mother who is also a Foe Destroyer is the worst.

### 4. LYING

Object — a person other than oneself.

Thought — the intention to deceive others, being motivated by the wish to speak of what one has or has not seen.

Action — an expression of body or speech.

Delusion — any of the three poisons in general.

Completion— occurs when the other person has understood what is meant.

Here the action does not only include expressions and deceptions of speech, but also lying through physical gestures.

There are three kinds of lies: those concerning superhuman attainments, such as claiming to have attained higher qualities than one has, which constitutes a defeat; great lies which bring benefit or harm to self and others; and petty lies bringing neither

19

benefit nor harm. Of all lies, those deprecating the Buddha or deceiving gurus and parents are the worst.

### 5. DIVISIVE SPEECH

Object — other people living in harmony.
Thought — the wish to divide them.
Action — to begin to do so.
Delusion — hatred in particular and the three poisons in general.
Completion— when the purpose is accomplished.

When those who are in conflict are attempting to unite, to try to divide them again by thought or action is also included here.

There are three kinds of divisive speech: forceful slander which divides friends directly; hinting, which divides through insinuation; and speech which divides through underhandedness. Of the varieties of divisive speech, that which separates a guru and disciple or causes a schism in the spiritual community is the worst.

### 6. HARSH WORDS

Object — the mind of a sentient being.
Thought — the wish to speak unpleasantly.
Action — to make effort in it.
Delusion — hatred in particular and the three poisons in general.
Completion— the actual expression in speech.

There are three categories of harsh words: rough speech directly exposing the bad qualities of others; speaking roughly by implication, mixing harsh words with jokes; and oblique rough speech, telling others of their friends' bad qualities. Of the varieties of harsh words, those spoken to parents and superiors are the worst.

### 7. IDLE CHATTER

Object — the mind of a sentient being.
Thought — the wish to chatter incessantly without care.
Action — to begin to voice songs, flattery and so forth.
Delusion — ignorance in particular and the three poisons in general.
Completion— the actual expression in speech.

There are three kinds of idle chatter: mistaken speech, such as the recitations of the Heterodox; nonsense like worldly gossip; and uselessly speaking the truth, such as teaching the doctrine to an inappropriate vessel. Of the varieties of idle gossip, that which distracts those who aspire solely towards the Dharma is the worst.

### 8. COVETOUSNESS

| | | |
|---|---|---|
| Object | — | the material possessions or the inner qualities of others. |
| Thought | — | wishing and hoping for others' wealth and possessions. |
| Action | — | to think of it repeatedly. |
| Delusion | — | attachment in particular and the three poisons in general. |
| Completion | — | to perform the action repeatedly, abandoning shame and embarrassment, and not to apply antidotes. |

There are three kinds of covetousness: attachment to class and family lineage, which is to covet what is one's own; attachment to others' wealth, which is to covet what belongs to others; and wishing for treasure beneath the earth, which is to covet what is neither. Of the varieties of covetousness, to covet the possessions of a renunciate is the worst.

### 9. MALICE

| | | |
|---|---|---|
| Object | — | the mind of a sentient being. |
| Thought | — | the wish to harm by killing or beating. |
| Action | — | the duration of the thought. |
| Delusion | — | hatred in particular and the three poisons in general. |
| Completion | — | to see this thought as worthy and to wish not to apply antidotes. |

There are three kinds of malice: wishing to kill others in battle and so forth is malice arising from hatred; wishing to harm rivals is malice arising from jealousy; and wishing to harm those associated in harmony is malice arising from resentment. Of the varieties of malice, to be motivated by relentless thoughts of harm is the worst.

## 10. WRONG VIEW

Object — wholesome or unwholesome doctrines.
Thought — the view that virtues and faults do not exist and the view that causality is distorted.
Action — the duration of this repeated thought.
Delusion — stupidity in particular and the three poisons in general.
Completion — to affirm that view and not apply an antidote.

There are three kinds of wrong view: not to accept that wholesome and unwholesome actions are the cause of joy and suffering respectively is the wrong view of causality; not to accept the attainment of true cessation through the practice of the true path is the wrong view of the Three Jewels of Refuge; wrong view is the worst of all unwholesome actions of the mind.

Abandoning these 10 unwholesome deeds is called ethics eliminating the 10 unwholesome actions.

### The Ethics of Individual Liberation.

Individual liberation is so called because thereby an individual becomes free from the suffering of cyclic existence. By nature it is a precept received with a motivating wish to achieve definite release from cyclic existence; not merely a prayer for goodness or protection from fears, but aspiration for peace for oneself. The ethics of individual liberation are to abandon harming others as well as the primary and secondary thoughts to do so. If the ethics of individual liberation are classified according to the holder, Vasubandhu says:

> Within the four general categories,
> there are eight kinds of individual liberation.

These are: the lay person's one-day vow, both layman's and laywoman's vows, both the male and female novice vows, the probationary nun vow and both the fully ordained monk and nun vows. These are the eight classes of individual liberation vows.

There are eight precepts to be observed within the lay person's one-day vow, and five layman or woman's general precepts. A novice has 36 precepts of observation and abandonment, including the minor faults to be avoided. On top of the novice's precepts, a probationary nun has six root and six secondary doctrines, 12 precepts in all, which she must observe. A fully ordained monk must observe 253 precepts which include four defeats, 13 remainders, 30 propelling downfalls, 90 solitary downfalls, four individual confessions and 112 faults. A fully ordained nun must observe 364 precepts, which include eight defeats, 20 remainders, 33 propelling downfalls, 180 solitary downfalls, 11 individual confessions and 112 faults.

The first of the eight categories of individual liberation, the lay person's one-day vow, is efficacious because it is observed for the duration of one day. The remaining seven must be observed until death, for they are received for the duration of this life. The recipient of these vows should be free from such hindrances as being obstructed from generating the vows by having performed a boundless action; not receiving the permission of one's ruler or parents, which hinders maintaining the vow; being unable to drive away crows, which is the hindrance of immaturity; and not having "golden hair and a pretty nose" which indicates that inordinate beauty is a hindrance. Apart from these, no distinction is made between those of high or low class, the rich or the poor; one may receive the vows if one is able to practise them according to one's mental capacity.

There are two traditions for receiving the vows that have not been taken previously; the earlier system which does not require much elaboration, and the present system requiring great complexity.

There are five ways to observe vows once they have been received:

### 1. Observation Dependent Upon Another Person:

To observe the vows, rely on the instructions of learned masters and take the good practices of monks as an example. After receiving full ordination in particular one must be under the care of a fully qualified resident master.

### 2. Observation Through the Purity of One's Own Thought:

Guard the vows by taking joyful interest in what is to be observed and what abandoned, being careful and conscientious about what is to be engaged in and what avoided through mindfulness and alertness in examining one's own mind, and through not losing a sense of embarrassment in relation to others or shame in relation to self.

### 3. Observation Through Recognition of Unfavourable Circumstances:

Recognising the causes of giving up vows, the causes of their degeneration, the conditions for preserving them and the causes which hinder clarity of the mind. This, in brief, is the training of hearing and contemplation as explained in the texts on discipline.

### 4. Observation Through Engagement in Perfect Training and Practice:

This is participation in the three basic ceremonies: the Confession Ceremony, the Rainy Season Retreat and the Ceremony of Lifting of Restrictions.

### 5. Observation While Dependent on the Conditions for a Happy Life:

It is necessary to observe the precepts by avoiding downfalls arising from dependence on clothes, food, utensils and dwellings. The main causes giving rise to faults, known as the four doors leading to downfalls, are ignorance, disrespect, carelessness and excessive delusion. The antidote to these is to rely on the five means of observing precepts and to make the same effort in observing ethics as one would make in guarding the orbs of one's eyes.

The vow of individual liberation is common to the ethics of both Mahayana and Hinayana. However, the Bodhisattva vow and the vow of the secret mantra belong to the ethics of the Mahayana only.

Having received the Bodhisattva vow, the precepts to be observed are 18 root downfalls and 56 faults. Having received the vow of secret mantra, the precepts to be observed are 14 root downfalls and eight secondary root downfalls, as well as many pledges and vows of the five Buddha-families in general and in particular. As specific delineation of the divisions of precepts of these two vows and the ways to observe them would be vast, they will not be explained here.

# CHAPTER FIVE

## *Training in Meditative Stabilisation*

The mind's abiding single-pointedly and without distraction on any virtuous object is what is known as meditative stabilisation. Through practice of it the actual formless absorptions and concentrations are achieved. Eventually, when we are thoroughly familiar with it, it becomes the perfection of concentration. Meditative stabilisation can be divided by nature into the mundane and the transcendent. In order to attain the latter the Bodhisattva Shantideva advises in his *Guide to the Bodhisattva's Way of Life*:

> Knowing that delusions are completely destroyed
> By special insight combined with calm abiding,
> Initially seek calm abiding
> Which arises from eager detachment from the world.

Thus, at the outset we should generate calm abiding and then special insight. Thereafter we must generate a meditative stabilisation which is a unification of calm abiding and special insight.

The reason for beginning with calm abiding meditation is that all the qualities of the three vehicles are the result of either concentrated or analytical meditation, which are either actual or approximate calmly abiding insight. If calm abiding has been attained then in any analytical meditation, whatever the particular object, the mind will dwell on it undistractedly. Thus, whatever virtuous practice we do will be powerful.

Concerning calm abiding meditation Arya Maitreya says in his *Discrimination of the Middle Way and the Extremes*:

> Applying the eight (antidotes) to eliminate the five
>     faults
> Is a cause for (calm abiding) to arise.

So, to eliminate the five faults the eight antidotes must be applied. The five faults are explained in the same text:

Laziness and forgetting the instructions,
Laxity and excitement,
Not applying and applying (antidotes),
Are stated to be five faults.

THE FIVE FAULTS

1. Laziness —This is a lack of interest in meditative stabilisation.
2. Forgetting the instructions —Whatever the object of meditation may be, it slips from one's attention because of forgetfulness.
3. Laxity and excitement—The object of meditation is not forgotten, but the mind is under the sway of either laxity or excitement.
4. Non-application —Although (the mind) is recognised to be under such sway, the antidotes to remedy it are not applied.
5. (Over) application —To apply the antidotes to laxity and excitement when neither of them is present, so that the mind is not focussed properly on the object, is the fifth fault.

Having eliminated these, we must meditate. The way to eliminate them by applying the eight antidotes is explained in the same text:

Abiding and that on which to abide,
Are the very cause and result.
By not forgetting the object,
Recognising laxity and excitement
And making strong applications to eliminate them,
Engage properly in pacification.

There are four antidotes to laziness, the first of the five faults, and one for each of the others.

The four antidotes to laziness are: faith, aspiration, effort and pliancy.

Mindfulness is the antidote to forgetfulness.

Introspection is the antidote to laxity and excitement.

Wishing to employ a remedy is the antidote to not applying antidotes.

Accurate equanimity is the remedy for over-application of antidotes.

(FIG. 1) FAULTS OF MEDITATIVE STABILISATION AND THEIR ANTIDOTES

| Five Faults | Eight Antidotes |
|---|---|
| | faith |
| | aspiration |
| laziness ———————— | effort |
| | pliancy |
| forgetfulness ——————— | mindfulness |
| (non-recognition of) | |
| laxity and excitement ——— | introspection |
| non-application (of antidotes)— | application |
| (over) application ————— | equanimity |

These eight must be applied in meditation. If we meditate knowing how they are divided among the nine stages of setting the mind, the way those are achieved through the six powers and how they are abbreviated as the four mental engagements, then a faultless meditative stabilisation will be attained spontaneously.

The nine stages of setting the mind are explained in Arya Maitreya's *Ornament for Mahayana Sutras*:

Focus the mind upon its object
Without distractions throughout its continuity;
Having quickly recognised a distraction
Patch it up again.
The wise will progressively
Concentrate the mind within
And thereby see its quality.
Having tamed the mind in meditative stabilisation
The faults of distractions are seen.
Being dissatisfied, pacify them;
Likewise pacify attachment, mental disturbance etc.,
As soon as they arise.
Thus, attainment will arise spontaneously
For the vow-holder who strictly applies the antidotes.
Having gained familiarity, there is no application.

## THE NINE STAGES OF SETTING THE MIND ARE:

1. Setting the mind
2. Continuous setting
3. Patch-like setting
4. Close setting
5. Disciplining
6. Pacifying
7. Thorough pacifying
8. Making single-pointed
9. Setting in equipoise.

## THE SIX POWERS ARE:

1. Power of hearing
2. Power of thinking
3. Power of mindfulness
4. Power of introspection
5. Power of effort
6. Power of complete familiarity.

## THE FOUR MENTAL ENGAGEMENTS ARE:

1. Forcible engagement
2. Interrupted engagement
3. Uninterrupted engagement
4. Effortless engagement.

At the beginning the first power is applied simply by listening to the instructions on how to set the mind on the object. That is followed by preventing the mind from being distracted by external objects and concentrating it within, focusing it upon its object. In this way the first stage, called setting the mind, arises. At that time the mind is unable to abide steadily upon its object and conceptions occur continuously, one after another, like a steep mountain water-fall. This gives rise to the experience of recognising conceptions, so that one may wonder, "Aren't these conceptions multiplying?" but it is simply that they were not recognised previously because the mind was not controlled from within. Applying mindfulness at this time is like an inquisitive traveller on a broad road, which is not a fault.

Having meditated steadily, there next arises the power of

thinking, the second power. In the course of practice of contemplation the mind is repeatedly focused upon its object. After some time, when this can be extended further, the second stage, called continuous setting, is reached. At that time there occurs an experience of having subdued mental conceptions; sometimes they are pacified, sometimes they arise turbulently. During these two stages of setting the mind both laxity and excitement are excessively strong while mental concentration is weak, and so firm efforts must be made to focus the mind on its object, thereby engaging the first of the four mental engagements, forcible engagement.

Next, through the third power, the power of mindfulness, whenever the mind is distracted from its object to another, it is recognised immediately and the mind is re-settled upon the original object. This gradually gives rise to the third stage called patch-like setting of the mind. Subsequently, through generating strong mindfulness from the beginning, the mind will not be distracted from its object. Through repeatedly restraining the naturally diffuse mind, it becomes progressively more subtle, which gives rise to the fourth stage called close setting of the mind. Then, by means of the fourth power, the power of introspection, the results of being distracted by signs of mental conception and secondary delusions are recognised. When distraction by these two is restricted there is joy in thinking of the qualities of meditative stabilisation. This fifth stage is called the disciplining stage of setting the mind.

The recognition, through introspection, of the faults of mental distraction dissipates feelings of displeasure toward meditative stabilisation. Consequently there arises the sixth stage called pacifying the mind. Then, through the fifth power, the power of effort, even subtle thoughts of attachment, distraction, sloth or laxity etc., will be unattractive from the moment they occur and will be forcefully eliminated. Thus the seventh stage of thorough pacifying of the mind is reached.

During the five stages of setting the mind from the third to the seventh, although the mind abides firmly in meditative stabilisation, there are still interruptions from laxity and excitement and hence this is the period of interrupted engagement. Thereafter, if the power of mindfulness is applied with effort and produced continuously, meditative stabilisation cannot be interrupted by negative forces such as laxity and excitement. Thus arises the eighth stage of the mind called making the mind single-pointed. At this juncture, if one makes continued efforts one will not be interrupted by laxity or excitement and will be able to maintain the session for longer. This is the period of uninterrupted engagement. Then, having meditated steadily, through the power of complete familiarity, the sixth power, it will not be necessary to make effort to apply mindfulness, for the mind will dwell on its object spontaneously. In this way the ninth stage, called setting the mind in equipoise, is reached. As an illustration of this point, one who has a very strong familiarity with reciting texts is well motivated at the beginning, but as soon as he starts is subject to intermittent mental distraction, yet his recitation continues effortlessly. Likewise, although at first the mind is focused upon its object with mindfulness, once it is evenly set it is unnecessary to apply mindfulness further and one will be able to practise meditative stabilisation spontaneously and continuously for a long time. This is the period of effortless engagement. Thus, when the mind engages incessantly in effortless meditative stabilisation, the ninth stage of setting the mind, a similitude of calm abiding, is obtained.

(FIG.2) STAGES AND FACTORS IN ACHIEVING CALM ABIDING.

| Six powers | Nine stages of setting the mind | Four mental engagements |
|---|---|---|
| hearing | 1. setting the mind | forcible engagement |
| thinking | 2. continuous setting | |
| mindfulness | 3. patch-like setting | |
| | 4. close setting | |
| introspection | 5. disciplining | interrupted engagement |
| | 6. pacifying | |
| effort | 7. thorough pacifying | |
| | 8. making single-pointed | uninterrupted engagement |
| complete familiarity | 9. setting in equipoise | effortless engagement |

Prior to this there was a slight experience of pliancy; as it gradually develops, this produces a mental pliancy which pacifies impediments to whatever mental virtues one wishes to do. When, by dint of that, one is freed from physical obstructions, physical pliancy is generated, the nature of which resembles an appealing object of touch. When pliancy is produced there is an experience of great physical bliss and consequently there is an unsurpassable experience of joy and bliss in the mind. With time the mind's experience of joy gradually wanes, the mind dwells firmly on the object and a stable pliancy is attained, which is a similitude of meditative stablisation. Simultaneously calm abiding conjoined with the preparatory stage of the first concentration is attained. Likewise, having established an actual calm abiding, through gradually familiarising the mind with it, one will attain the actual concentration of higher realms, having freed oneself from attachment to the lower of the three realms and nine levels. (The three realms are the desire realm, form realm and formless realm. The nine levels are the level of desire, the level of the first concentration, the level of the second concentration, the level of the third concentration and the level of the fourth concentration and the formless levels of infinite space, infinite consciousness, nothingness and peak of existence.)

The result of having meditated on the causal absorption in this way is to be born as a form or formless god. To begin with, the way to meditate on the causal absorption of concentration is explained in Acharya Asanga's *Compendium of Knowledge:*

> The absorption of the first concentration is gained through the seven mental contemplations. What are these seven mental contemplations? Mental contemplation perfectly aware of characteristics; that arising from belief; complete isolation; withdrawal or joy; analysis; final training and the mental contemplation of the fruit of final training.

So the preparations for the first concentration are the six mental contemplations: mental contemplation of knowledge of individual characteristics, mental contemplation of belief, mental contemplation of complete isolation, mental contemplation of withdrawal or joy, mental contemplation of analysis and mental contemplation of final training.

The first, mental contemplation of knowledge of individual characteristics, is to see the defects of the lower, desire realm and the qualities of the first concentration of the higher realm, which is

31

a rough understanding arising from careful analysis based on the combination of hearing and thinking. Mental contemplation arising from belief transforms that into the very nature of meditation. Mental contemplation produced by isolation eliminates the three sets of great, manifest desire-delusions by isolating them, then mental contemplation of withdrawal or joy eliminates the three sets of middling, manifest desire-delusions. Mental contemplation of analysis investigates and analyses whether the mind stream is stained by the three sets of desire-delusions or not.

(The nine sets of desire-delusions are the three sets of great desire-delusions, which are great, middling and small; the three sets of middling desire-delusions, which are great, middling and small and like wise, the three sets of small desire-delusions, which are great, middling and small.)

Mental contemplation of final training is similarly an analysis, which eliminates even the subtlest of the subtle of the three sets of small desire-delusions by the force of antidotes. In this way, the actual stage of the first concentration is attained, being the fruit of final training of the six mental contemplations. These view the lower realms as coarse and defective and higher realms as faultless and peaceful and, having both coarse and fine aspects, they are realisations common to both worldly and transcendent paths.

The actual stage of the first concentration has five branches; investigation and analysis are both antidotes, joy and bliss are both benefits, and the single-pointed mind is the basis. When it includes both investigation and analysis it is called the ordinary actual stage, and when there is analysis but no investigation it is called the special actual stage.

The preparation for the second concentration is to recognise the drawbacks of the first concentration and the flawless qualities of the second, through mental contemplation of knowledge of individual characteristics and so forth. When one is thereby freed from attachment to the first concentration, the second will be attained.

The actual stage of the second concentration has four branches, such as perfect clarity etc. Of these, internal clarity is an antidote, while joy and bliss, being produced from meditative stabilisation, are benefits. Meditative stabilisation itself is the branch of abiding. Here internal clarity refers to the mindfulness, introspection and equanimity of that very stage; because it has abandoned all internal conceptions it is called internal clarity.

The preparation for the third concentration is to recognise the drawbacks of the second concentration and the qualities of the third through the analysis of the six mental contemplations. When one is thereby freed from attachment to the second concentration, the actual stage of the third concentration will be attained. The actual stage of the third concentration has five branches: mindfulness, introspection and equanimity are antidotes, as joy has been abandoned bliss is the benefit, and meditative stabilisation is the branch of abiding.

The preparation for the fourth concentration is to recognise the drawbacks of the third concentration and the qualities of the fourth through the analysis of the six mental contemplations. When one is thereby freed from attachment to the third concentration the actual stage of the fourth concentration has four branches: perfect mindfulness and perfect equanimity are both antidotes, the feeling of equanimity is a benefit and meditative stabilisation is the branch of abiding. Here, perfect mindfulness refers to complete freedom from the eight faults of concentration, so it is free from both investigation and analysis, which resemble fire in relation to the first concentration; from the feelings of pleasure and pain, which arise concomitant with sense perception in relation to the second concentration; from the feelings of bliss and unhappiness, which arise concomitant with mental perception in relation to the third concentration, and from inhalation and exhalation in relation to the fourth concentration. The above branches of concentration are 18 in name, but 11 in actuality.

As Acharya Vasubandhu states in his *Treasury of Knowledge*:

> The first has five (branches), investigation, analysis,
> Joy, bliss and meditative stabilisation.
> The second has four branches,
> Clarity, joy etc.
> The third has five, equanimity,
> Mindfulness, introspection, bliss and abiding.
> The last has four, mindfulness, equanimity
> Neither bliss nor pain, meditative stabilisation.

The above concentrative absorptions are the result of having meditated on the small, medium and great actual stages of the first concentration, whereby one will be born in the abodes of the first concentration, Brahma type etc. Having perfected the small, medium and great actual stages of each concentration one will experience the ripened result of each abode, up to the abodes of the fourth concentration, cloudless etc., which is achieved by meditating on the small, medium and great actual stages of the fourth concentration. That ripened result is the apparent form born in each abode; the absorbed mind is the result congruent with its cause, and the apparent wealth of the place is the environmental result. Similarly, there are four respective sources of the formless realms: Infinite Space, Infinite Consciousness, Nothingness and Peak of Existence.

Once an undegenerated mind of the fourth concentration has been attained, by perfecting the meditation which curtails the awareness, vision and appearance of form and thinks of all phenomena as being as infinite as space, the absorption of infinite space will be actualised. Likewise, by perfecting the meditation that consciousness is also as infinite as space the absorption which is the source of infinite consciousness is achieved.

When both of the above are viewed as having signs, by perfecting meditation on the thought, 'there is nothing to be held', the absorption which is the source of nothingness is attained. Having then seen these three as having signs, and perfected meditation on the thought,'there is no gross perception but no lack of subtle perception', then the absorption of neither perception nor imperception is achieved, which is called the absorption of the Peak of Existence. The results of such formless absorptions are such that although there are no distinctions of abode according to gross form in the formless realms, yet there are distinctions with regard to superiority and inferiority, length of life, status and so forth. As meditative stabilisation becomes progressively vaster and firmer so life increases and the resultant bliss of high status becomes more exalted. Special qualities of the two higher realms, dependent on the actual stages of the four concentrations are the four immeasurables, love and so forth, and the five mundane clairvoyant powers: the divine eye, divine ear, knowledge of others' minds, recollection of past lives and knowledge of the migrations of death and birth.

Those who have set out on the paths of the three vehicles must

initially develop such meditative stabilisations and their qua...
followed by their special, higher attainments. Thus, clairvoyant
powers and so forth become the basis of all qualities.

In dependence upon the mind of the actual stages of the four
concentrations in particular, the absorption of imperception will be
attained and in reliance upon the mind of the actual stage of the
Peak of Existence, the absorption of cessation etc., is achieved.
These are to be aspired to and practised by both Buddhist and non-
Buddhists and are also the preliminaries for those who enter the
doctrine of the Conqueror gradually. Therefore, having understood this, one should train in the practice of familiarising oneself
with them.

# CHAPER SIX

## *Training in Wisdom*

The third of the higher trainings is of wisdom. Wisdom is the thorough discernment of phenomena through investigation and analysis. When comprehensive familiarity with that wisdom is gained, it transforms into the Perfection of Wisdom, of which there are three categories:

1. Wisdom understanding the ultimate—which is to understand the reality of selflessness either directly or through a generic image.
2. Wisdom understanding the conventional—which is to have mastery over the five fields of knowledge.
3. Wisdom understanding the welfare of sentient beings—which is knowledge of how to bring about the present and future welfare of sentient beings, without misdeeds.

Of these we must principally accomplish the wisdom of selflessness. In explaining the meaning of selflessness, there are different assertions amongst the various schools of Buddhist tenets, all of which become a means ultimately to understand the view of Prasangika-Madhyamika.

Here, I will explain largely in accordance with the Prasangika-Madhyamika school. Chandrakirti states:

> When his mind sees that all delusions and faults
> Arise from the view of the transitory collection,
> And he understands that the self is an object of that,
> The yogi negates the self.

Hence, the ignorance which is the conception of true existence along with its latencies is the root of all detriments to existence and peace, which can be uprooted by nothing other than the wisdom realising selflessness, whose mode of apprehension is directly contrary to it. Therefore, one should strive in the practice of the exalted special insight, which is the means to understand the meaning of selflessness.

There are two aspects of selflessness, that of persons and that of phenomena. If at first the selflessness of persons is discerned, the selflessness of phenomena will be easily understood; therefore the selflessness of persons should be established at the beginning.

This is also said in Acharya Shantarakshita's *Ornament for the Middle Way*:

> These existents asserted as self and others
> Are ultimately free from existence
> As one or many, and
> Hence lack inherent existence like a reflection.

It is therefore important to rely on the reasons for an object's being free from being one or many, which are qualified by the four essentials. The four essentials are:

> ascertaining the object of negation,
> ascertaining the pervasion,
> ascertaining freedom from being one, and
> ascertaining freedom from being many.

Acharya Shantideva said:

> Without finding the object under investigation
> Its lack of (inherent) existence will not be recognised.

In order to search for the meaning of selflessness it is very important to recognise the object of negation according to the manner in which it is apprehended by the conception of true existence. If we recognise only the gross object of negation and not the subtle, only the gross object of negation will be eliminated. Then traces of the object of negation will remain, because of which the conception of true existence will be unharmed and one will fall into an extreme of superimposition. If one defines the object of negation too broadly and everything which appears to the group of six consciousnesses is held to be an object of negation, one will fall into an extreme of undermining the nominal order. There is a grave danger of falling into an extreme of nihilistic views.

When one has carefully investigated, thinking, "How does the

innate conception of a self apprehend an inherently existent `I'?",
one discovers that it apprehends an `I' that exists independently of
the aggregates, which are its basis of imputation, without relying
on the collection of the five aggregates and so forth at all. This is the
way the innate conception of self apprehends the `I'. Recognising
this unmistakenly is the first essential, ascertaining the object of
negation.

If the 'I' were to exist inherently, it should be either of one
identity with, or separate from the aggregates which are the basis
of imputation, for there is no other mode of being than these two.
To be certain of this constitutes the second essential, ascertaining
the pervasion. If the self and aggregates were both of one nature,
truly or inherently, they would be quite inseparably one. The
reason is that for things to exist as one in nature, yet to appear as
opposite or of separate categories, that is, for their mode of appearance to be incongruent with their mode of being, is a conventional
fallacy. If they were truly existent, it would be impossible for the
modes of appearance and being to be incongruent, because to the
mind which apprehends true existence, the object must appear in
the way it exists. Thus, if the self and aggregates were truly one,
these absurd consequences would follow: a person would have as
many selves as he has aggregates, or, as there is but one self, so the
aggregates would become one; as the aggregates arose and disinte-
grated so the self would also arise and disintegrate. When one has
analysed logically in this way and understood that the self and
aggregates do not exist inherently as one, this is the third essential,
ascertaining their freedom from being one.

If both self and aggregates were inherently different, their
differences should withstand logical analysis, in which case they
should be different and unrelated in all respects, substance and so
forth. The reason is that for them to be different in their isolates
while being undifferentiable in nature is a false presentation, and is
consequently untenable if they are inherently existent.

However, if they were different and unrelated, this absurd
consequence would follow: when the aggregates experienced sickness, aging, disintegration and so forth, the self would not experience sickness, aging and so forth, therefore the self would not
possess the characteristics of the aggregates, such as birth and

decay. Moreover, if the aggregates were to be removed, one by one, the self would be revealed as the remainder.

The fourth essential, ascertaining their freedom from being many, is to affirm that self and aggregates are not different in an inherently existent manner. Likewise, the mind which understands that they do not exist inherently, neither as one nor different, understands the reasons which support the thesis establishing the lack of inherent existence. The way that the thesis of the self's lack of inherent existence is understood may be illustrated thus—having searched for a lost ox, which could have wandered in only two valleys, merely seeing that it is not at the far end, the middle or mouth of either valley, one will spontaneously generate the thought that the ox one has in mind cannot be found.

The mode of appearance of the object of negation to the conception of true existence, which was identified previously, is kept in mind and analysed as to whether it is free from being one or many. As soon as it is realised as free from being many and one thinks, 'The self to be negated, which has been called to mind, does not exist', when it has vanished into vacuity, the selflessness of persons will be understood and the middle view will be found.

Concerning the selflessness of phenomena the *King of Meditative Stabilisations Sutra* says:

> Just as you have recognised the self
> So mentally apply that knowledge to all;
> All phenomena are of this nature
> Completely pure like space.

The above explanation with respect to persons can similarly be applied to objects, a vase for example; it is produced in dependence on a substantial cause (the clay), which is a conglomeration of innumerable fine particles and the auxiliary conditions such as the skill of the craftsman's hands. Thus it is produced in dependence on many causes, conditions and dependent arisings. Apart from these, there is no independent vase, whose mode of existence is spontaneously arising and self-sufficient. Likewise, all phenomena are merely coexistents, arising dependent on causes, conditions, parts and so forth, other than which they have no inherent existence. Although they do not exist in that way, they appear to do so and the mind apprehends them according to that appearance, which is the apprehension of the self of phenomena.

Having recognised such a mind's mode of apprehension and completed analysis by means of the four essentials, such as the essential of ascertaining the object of negation, as explained above, the object of such apprehension appears to the mind as vanishing into vacuity and as being a mere name, existing as merely imputed to the collection of dependent arisings: then one will have realized the selflessness of phenomena.

Likewise, through the force of understanding that both self and phenomena lack inherent existence, one generates a strong conviction that the system of the working of cause and effect is a mere dependent imputation. Then, contingent on the certainty that dependent arising is merely imputed by name, there arises a cogent certainty about the emptiness of independent existence, which has been explained as understanding that emptiness means dependent arising and dependent arising means emptiness. Such is the understanding of the correct view, the unsurpassed thought of Buddha.

Freedom from being one or many as just explained is not the only reasoning which is a means to understand emptiness, for there are numerous others, such as the reasons known as diamond slivers, the reasons negating existent and nonexistent production, the reasons negating the four possibilities of production and the reasons for dependent arising.

When one has correctly understood the meaning of selflessness, which is profound emptiness, by means of many such reasons, to then practise analytical and concentrated meditation on it more intensely is the way to practise the training in higher wisdom.

# CHAPTER SEVEN

## *Ascending the Path of Hearers and Solitary Realisers by Relying on the Three Trainings*

Relying upon the practice of the three higher trainings, as explained above, some travel the path of the Hinayana and achieve the final liberation of Hearers and Solitary Realisers, the state of Foe Destroyer, while others travelling the path of the Mahayana achieve Buddhahood. Of the two paths of the Hinayana, those of Hearers and Solitary Realisers, the first, that of Hearers, consists of five paths: the path of accumulation, the path of preparation, the path of seeing, the path of meditation and the path of no more learning. Chandrakirti explains how to advance upon them in his *Seventy Verses on the Three Refuges:*

> If you set out for a particular liberation
> And always engage in virtue,
> While striving towards the goal of Hearers,
> You will gradually become a Hearer.

(Cylic existence is an instant in the continuity of the contaminated aggregates in the cycle of births, which means involuntarily taking birth by force of action and delusion from the Peak of Existence to the Most Tortuous Hell.)

Having realised actually how we are tortured by the three sufferings of cyclic existence, we develop a wish for freedom from it. When we have generated an experience of uncontrived interest in liberation for ourselves, we have entered the Hearers' path of accumulation, which has three sections, small, medium and great. At this time practitioners meditate on ugliness and develop meditative stabilisation through attention to inhalation and exhalation of breath. They develop close mindfulness, perfect abandonments and the legs of miracles etc. Through the power of these meditations they overcome the misapprehension of suffering as being clean, joyful, permanent or having a self, as well as overcoming delusions such as attachment and hatred. Taking no interest at all in the wealth or marvels of cyclic existence, they have the qualities required to proceed directly towards impeccable liberation. They can perform miracles and so forth as they wish and can employ any of the five clairvoyant powers. Subsequently, during the path of preparation all the qualities of the path of accumulation become more enhanced than before.

The path of preparation consists of four levels: heat, peak, forbearance, and supreme mundane qualities. At each of these levels superior insight is gradually attained, which derives from meditation and contemplation of the reality of the Four Noble Truths. Thereby arises an especially clear view of the general meaning of such aspects as impermanence, suffering, emptiness and selflessness. Inconceivable qualities are attained such as the five faculties and five powers. When practitioners progress from the level of supreme mundane qualities of the path of preparation to the path of seeing, through direct insight into the 16 attributes of the Four Noble Truths, they sever at the root all the 112 delusions of the three realms to be abandoned on the path of seeing and, attaining the qualities of a Superior, they become the ultimate Sangha (aspirant to virtue) refuge. Having reached the path of seeing, they will engage in prolonged meditation on that reality which they have already understood directly in accordance with the Eightfold Noble Path in order to crush the seeds of innate delusions.

The noble path of definite release consists of : right view, right thought, right speech, right conduct, right livelihood, right mindfulness, and right meditative stabilisation. Their nature and function are as follows:

Right view — is to discern the view through analytical means in the post-meditational period, thinking, 'This is what I have realised during meditative equipoise to be the reality of the Four Noble Truths.'

Right thought — is to examine how the profound meaning already understood through correct reasons and signs complies with the meaning

|                              | of the sutras, so that its significance may be understood and explained to others. |
|------------------------------|---|
| Right speech —               | is to show others, by means of teaching, debate and writing, the nature of reality free from elaboration as it is represented conventionally by mere words, and to lead them to the conviction that it is the perfect view. This is pure speech free from deceit etc. |
| Right conduct —              | is pure behaviour convincing others that all our activities conform with the doctrine and are harmonious with pure ethics. |
| Right livelihood—            | is to convince others that our livelihood is proper, not mixed with the evil fruits of wrong livelihood and free from wheedling behaviour, flattering speech and so forth. |
| Right effort —               | is to meditate repeatedly on the meaning of reality that has already been seen, which is thereby an antidote to the delusions to be abandoned on the path of meditation. |
| Right mindful- — ness        | is to retain the object of calm abiding and insight meditation without forgetting it, which acts as an antidote to the secondary delusion forgetfulness. |
| Right meditative— stabilisation | is to establish meditative stabilisation free from the faults of laxity and excitement, which acts as an antidote to hindrances and leads to the progressive attainment of the qualities of the path. |

These may also be condensed into four, as Arya Maitreya's text *Discrimination of the Middle Way and the Extremes* says:

Complete severing and indication,
Three aspects to convince others
And antidotes to hindrances
Are these eight branches of the path.

Right view is complete severance, right thought is an indicator, right speech, conduct and livelihood are to convince others, while the remaining three are antidotes.

When, in dependence upon meditation on the meaning of suchness as already realised, the direct antidotes to the major delusions to be abandoned on the path of meditation are produced, the path of meditation is attained.

There are two kinds of abandonment, gradual and simultaneous. According to the gradual system, abandonment entails giving up the nine sets of delusions of the desire realm to be eliminated on the path of meditation, starting from the gross level. Up to the successive abandonment of the nine sets of delusions to be eliminated at the Peak of Existence, there are 81 objects to be given up by applying their antidotes, of which the weakest are produced first. Finally, when practitioners attain the path of thorough liberation resulting from immutable meditative stabilisation on the path of meditation, they attain the path of no more learning of a Hearer, or the Hearer's state of Foe Destroyer.

According to the simultaneous system, the nine great, major delusions to be abandoned on the path of meditation within the three realms and nine levels are abandoned simultaneously. Likewise, from the abandonment of the nine middling, major delusions to the simultaneous abandonment of the nine small, minor delusions the practitioner ascends the path and attains that state of Foe Destroyer.

Concerning the Solitary Realiser's path of the Hinayana, Chandrakirti's work *The Seventy Verses on the Three Refuges* says:

> He who wishes for self-generated wisdom
> And is interested in a Solitary Realiser's enlighten-
>     ment
> Strives in this way and attains
> The enlightenment of a Solitary Realiser alone.

So there is a difference of interest in enlightenment, and in the number of aeons when merits are accumulated and those when they are not; otherwise the presentation of the five paths is largely similar to those of the Hearers.

# CHAPTER EIGHT

## *The Mahayana Perfection Vehicle*

The Mahayana consists of both the perfection vehicle and the secret mantra, vajra vehicle. Firstly, the path of the perfection vehicle which, like the paths of the Hinayana, also consists of five paths such as the path of accumulation.

When one generates an uncontrived aspiration for enlightenment, motivated by compassion and love, taking responsibility upon oneself to provide benefit and joy for all sentient beings who lack happiness and are tortured by sufferings, one will become a Bodhisattva, a Son of the Conqueror, a great being, a universal object of devotion of all gods, humans and other beings, and will attain the Mahayana path of accumulation. As soon as one generates such a mind of enlightenment one gains infinite qualities such as purification of numerous unwholesome downfalls and the swift collection of merit and insight. During the great path of accumulation, relying on the actual stage of concentration one attains clairvoyance by which one can visit Buddha-fields in the 10 directions and honour the many Buddhas there. Then, through the strength of one's attainment of the meditative stabilisation of the stream of Dharma, one hears countless profound and extensive teachings from the Buddhas and practises them. By contemplating a generic image of emptiness, that all phenomena are empty of true existence, one attains the path of preparation, which is a combination of calm abiding and insight.

The path of preparation has four levels: heat, peak, forbearance and supreme mundane qualities. At each level the gross dualistic conception of true existence becomes more subtle and an increasing clarity of the generic image of emptiness arises, which thereby subdues conceptions apprehending the true existence of subject and object.

Due to one's extensive practice of method and wisdom throughout the day and night, even in one's dreams, one sees all phenomena as lacking inherent existence, like an apparition. One takes no interest in the Hinayana, but is eager in expounding the doctrine to sentient beings and so forth. One gains the signs of attaining the peak level of the path of preparation, such as ability to pacify harm arising from the four elements and other kinds of harmful interference such as sickness and so forth.

The Bodhisattva with sharp intelligence who gains the signs of irreversibility from complete enlightenment while on the path of preparation has qualities magnificent beyond words. Then, through direct insight into emptiness on the uninterrupted path of the Mahayana path of seeing, the seeds of both the 108 intellectually derived delusive obstructions of the three realms and the 112 intellectually derived obstructions to omniscience are abandoned simultaneously. When one attains such a path of seeing, one leaves behind the sufferings of birth, sickness and death which are impelled by actions and delusions. On accomplishing the meditative stabilisation known as "blissfully going over all phenomena", no matter what hostile conditions one may meet with, such as poison, weapons or fire, one experiences only joy and is unaffected by suffering.

From the first to the 10th Bodhisattva ground, which constitute the path of meditation, one gradually abandons the seeds of the 16 delusions as well as the 108 obstructions to omniscience to be abandoned on the path of meditation, starting from the gross level, and progressively acquires qualities to overcome hostile factors.

### THE TEN GROUNDS:

1. The Very Joyful
2. The Stainless
3. The Luminous
4. The Radiant
5. The Very Difficult to Overcome
6. The Approaching
7. The Gone Afar
8. The Immovable
9. The Good Intelligence
10. The Cloud of Doctrine.

For aeons upon each of these 10 grounds one honours many millions of Buddhas by means of one's extensive special thought and upholds the holy doctrine, maturing countless sentient beings through the four means of assembling disciples. The complete training, special signs, features and so forth of each ground have qualities beyond thought and expression.

Finally, having gradually ascended the 10 grounds the continuity of the subtle obstructions to omniscience is severed in the last moment of the uninterrupted path concluding the 10th ground. Then the state of Buddha, endowed with infinite qualities, will be attained.

# CHAPTER NINE

## *The Secret Mantra, Vajra Vehicle*

Acharya Tripitakamala's *Lamp for the Three Modes* says:

> Having the same object, but clearly defined,
> Having many methods, but no difficulties,
> Designed for those with sharp intelligence
> The mantra vehicle is superior.

Thus, this is superior to the perfection vehicle, yet there is no difference in the quality or status of the enlightenment which is the ultimate result attained by both the mantra and the perfection vehicles. The distinction between these two vehicles lies in their different means of attaining the consummate state of a Buddha. As the consummate Buddha body consists of both a truth body and form body, they must each have their own exclusive causes. According to both sutra and mantra alike, the mind of enlightenment conjoined with the wisdom understanding emptiness is the exclusive cause of the truth body and an auxiliary condition of the form body. The secret mantra vajra vehicle has extensive means acting as exclusive causes of the form body; the perfection vehicle, lacking those, has only the means of generating the mind of enlightenment and the six perfections. For this reason, relying on the perfection vehicle Buddhahood may be attained, not in a single life, but in the course of many lifetimes. Relying on the path of secret mantra those of superior intelligence can attain enlightenment in one life or even a few years and thus secret mantra's special quality is its swiftness.

What is this exclusive cause of the form body which is a special quality of the secret mantra, vajra vehicle? It is the incomparable method of deity yoga, meditating on a similitude of the features, abode and so forth, of the result and form body, which is an extensive method not possessed by the perfection vehicle.

As Chapter 13 of the *Vajrapanjara Tantra* says:

> Secret mantra consists of
> Action tantras for the inferior,
> Yoga without actions for those above them,
> Excellent Yoga for supreme sentient beings,
> And Highest Yoga for those above them.

There are four sets of root tantras which accord with the intelligence of the disciples to be trained, each of which contains many sub-divisions. There are also many differences among them according to the nature of the paths, their categories, the ways in which they are explained in tantric texts and their speed. However, as the finer details can only be revealed secretly to those disciples who are vessels of a continuum which has been ripened through empowerment and entry into the mandala of the vajra vehicle, it is not permissible to hawk them in the market as one pleases. As it is inappropriate to do so here, I shall say no more.

In brief, the general practice of secret mantra may be summarised in this way: it should be practised by a person who has gained experience of the common paths, such as the wish for definite freedom and the mind of enlightenment. If one does not meet these qualifications one should at least be acquainted with these practices. At the outset one should receive initiation into the mandala of any class of tantra from a qualified master. Thus, taking the safeguarding of the vows and pledges as a foundation, through single-pointedly concentrating on the visualised mandala of the deity one establishes the form body of a resultant Buddha. Next, in reliance upon the skilful means of identifying the internal winds, channels, elements and so forth, one engages in the yoga of entering into the sphere of the great seal of clear light free from elaborations and attains the wisdom truth body of a Buddha.

# CHAPTER TEN

## The Four Bodies, Qualities and Virtuous Activity of a Consummate Buddha

Relying upon the paths of sutra and mantra as explained above, a Buddha's body is attained, as Arya Maitreya's *Ornament for Clear Realisations* says:

> Nature body, complete enjoyment body
> And similarly the others, emanation body,
> Truth body, as well as its deeds,
> Are perfectly explained in four aspects.

There are four bodies: nature body, wisdom truth body, enjoyment body and emanation body.

### 1. NATURE BODY

The obstructions to omniscience are completely abandoned by immutable meditative stabilisation in the last moment of the 10 grounds on the path of meditation, and when by such an uninterrupted path the stage of thorough liberation is attained all adventitious defilements, the two obstructions, are abandoned. That cessation is the attainment of the nature body free from adventitious defilements.

The very emptiness of true existence of the mind which formerly, at the ordinary level, was known as the naturally abiding Buddha-nature, is finally raised to perfection, becoming the emptiness of the omniscient mind of a Buddha, which is known as the nature body. It appears only when Buddhahood is attained; yet it is not impermanent, but, being compounded by causes and conditions and of unchangeable nature, it is naturally permanent.

### 2. WISDOM TRUTH BODY

To know all objects of knowledge and all phenomena whatever, directly, as if they were in front of one, is omniscient wisdom. If it is divided according to its isolate there are 21 classifications of uncontaminated wisdom from the 37 classes of phenomena directed towards enlightenment up to omniscience. These will be classified below, when the qualities of mind are explained. The nature body and wisdom truth body are only directly accessible to Buddhas amongst themselves.

### 3. COMPLETE ENJOYMENT BODY

This is known as the basis of emanation for the supreme emanation body. It is by nature a form body possessing the five certainties of a Buddha and is first gained in the richly adorned Highest Pure Land (Akanishta), which is produced by force of meditation on the purification of the field during the path of training.

The five certainties which qualify the form body are:

1. Certainty of place: he abides only in the richly adorned Highest Pure land.
2. Certainty of body: he is perfectly and clearly adorned by the 32 noble signs and the 80 noble marks.
3. Certainty of attendants: he is surrounded by an exclusive host of Bodhisattva superiors, and can be seen neither by ordinary people, nor by hearers or solitary realiser foe destroyers.
4. Certainty of doctrine: he teaches only the Mahayana doctrine and not that of the Hinayana.
5. Certainty of time: he remains without manifesting birth and death until the exhaustion of cyclic existence.

The enjoyment body is accessible to the superiors of the Mahayana who have seen truth directly.

### 4. EMANATION BODY

This is the form body which lacks the five certainties, but which can be seen by ordinary disciples. There are three kinds, the supreme emanation body, the artisan emanation and personified emanation body.

The supreme emanation body, whose basis of emanation is the enjoyment body, fulfils the purposes of disciples through performance of the 12 deeds in this world and various other worldly realms. The emanation body is identified by its adornment of signs and marks, an example of which is our teacher Buddha Shakyamuni himself. Similarly, the 12 deeds are also exemplified by those of Buddha Shakyamuni.

The 12 deeds are:

1. The descent from the Joyful Abode (Tushita).
2. Entry into the mother's womb.
3. Taking birth in the Lumbini garden.
4. Displaying skill in the worldly arts and youthful sports.
5. The amusements of a prince in the company of queens.
6. Becoming ordained as a result of the distress of going to the four doors of the city.
7. Engaging in austere practices for six years by the Nairanjana River.
8. Approaching and sitting beneath the Bodhi tree.
9. Defeating all malevolent forces.
10. Becoming a completely perfect Buddha on the full moon day of fourth month.
11. Turning the wheel of doctrine of the Four Noble Truths on the fourth day of the sixth month.
12. Passing away in the city of Kushinagar.

To the eyes of ordinary disciples some of these deeds, as performed, appeared to be those of a Bodhisattva and some the deeds of a Buddha. Yet, because the Buddhas are skilled in the means of training disciples, they were only a demonstration, for in fact all the deeds from the descent from the Joyful Abode up to the 12th are without exception deeds of a Buddha.

An example of the artisan emanation body is that emanated by Buddha Shakyamuni in the form of a musician (lute player) in order to tame the king of celestial musicians, Raja Pramudita. An instance of the personified emanation body is the son of a god, Svetaketu, in the Joyful Abode.

Of the four bodies of a Buddha, the nature body and wisdom truth body cannot be seen by ordinary disciples. Both types of form body, the enjoyment body and emanation body appear directly to disciples and perform extensive deeds to benefit wandering beings.

The bodies of a Buddha can be classified in various ways such as the division into four bodies explained above. However, of these four both the nature body and the wisdom truth body may be treated as one, called the truth body, within a classification of three bodies, the truth, enjoyment and emanation bodies. Also, the enjoyment and emanation bodies can be treated as one form body, so there is also a classification into two bodies, the truth and form bodies.

Although there are many ways to classify the qualities of a resultant Buddha, they may be explained with respect to his body, speech, mind and virtuous activity.

The qualities of the body are the signs and marks. The 32 signs of a great person include golden wheels like very clear bright embossed designs on the palms of hands and soles of feet and so forth. The 80 good marks include the bright reddish copper-coloured nails of the hands and feet, the charming complexion and so forth. The mere sight of this beautiful body wholly embellished by such ornaments has the ability to implant special seeds of liberation. The nature of each of the signs and marks is of the same entity as omniscient wisdom, unlike our own contaminated aggregates, and therefore each sign and mark and every single hair also has a direct view of all phenomena.

In fields throughout the 10 immeasurable directions the Buddha manifests various miraculous physical emanations simultaneously. In some he demonstrates taking birth, in others the turning of the wheel of doctrine, in some he shows the way to train in Bodhisattva deeds and in others the manner of passing away. Thus he leads sentient beings along the good path by performing deeds according to the needs of those to be tamed. A single hair-pore of his body contains the three times and can clearly reveal all the activities of the path of training.

The qualities of his speech are such that its mellifluent sound generates and enhances roots of virtue in the minds of others according to each individual's disposition and aspiration. His soothing voice brings joy to the minds of listeners upon their merely hearing it and is attractive to the mind in that it reveals the profound meaning of the two truths, dependent arising and so forth, and thus each holy word pleases the mind. Even a single utterance perfectly contains all the qualities of the 64 rhythms of his voice. Furthermore, in an assembly of gods, nagas, humans, birds, animals etc., even one pronouncement of the Tathagata can be understood by each being in his own language, dispelling his doubts and so forth. Such are the qualities of his speech.

Amongst the qualities of mind, the qualities of knowledge consist of 21 categories of uncontaminated wisdom. Omitting those categories shared with Hearers and Solitary Realisers, the exclusive qualities of a Buddha are:

The 10 Powers:

1. Knowledge of proper and improper vessels.
2. Knowledge of actions and their consequences.
3. Knowledge of concentration and the doors of liberation etc.
4. Knowledge of superior and inferior faculties.
5. Knowledge of various aspirations.
6. Knowledge of the classifications into 18 constituents etc.
7. Knowledge of paths leading to all existence and peace.
8. Knowledge recollecting past lives.
9. Knowledge of birth and death.
10. Knowledge of the exhaustion of contamination.

The Four Fearlessnesses:

1. The assurance of having attained the excellent insight of direct knowledge of all phenomena for the purpose of self.
2. The assurance of having attained the excellent abandonment, having exhausted all obstructions.
3. The assurance of the postponement of his own liberation through attachment to the aims of others.
4. The assurance that the path comprehending the reality of the Four Noble Truths is a path of liberation.

These assurances concordant with the doctrine cannot be defeated by any challenger.

The Three Close Mindfulnesses:

1. Abandonment of attachment to those disciples who listen respectfully to his teaching.
2. Abandonment of disdain for the angry and disrespectful.
3. Abandonment of both attachment and disdain for those with a mixed attitude.

The three undeceitful attitudes are not to have the thought, "I will conceal these faults from others' notice," with respect to the three doors of action.

A feature of fearlessness is to abide always in close mindfulness, while engaging in virtuous activities of body and speech for the welfare of others. Has completely eradicated all delusions and obstructions to omniscience, as well as their instincts and great compassion is directed continuously, both day and night, towards placing all people in benefit and joy, thinking, "Who is to be tamed?"

There are 18 qualities of the Buddha not shared with Hearers and Solitary Realisers:

Six qualities of behaviour:

1. While going from town to town or to isolated places, he is not disturbed by fear of thieves, robbers or tigers etc.
2. He does not babble with laughter through force of instinct, nor exclaim loudly because of wrong paths.
3. His mindfulness does not degenerate in the way that an action is inadvertently forgotten over a period of time.
4. He remains in mental equipoise on the meaning of emptiness constantly, whether he is engaged in meditative absorption or not.
5. He does not have the thought which clings to discriminations between disharmonious cyclic existence and the peaceful state beyond death (nirvana).
6. He is not indifferent to sentient beings in neglecting their aims or failing to examine carefully the time to train them.

Six qualities of insight:

7. Love and compassion give rise to his uninterrupted yearning to fulfil the aims of sentient beings.
8. He will eagerly go to Buddha-fields more numerous than

the sand grains of the Ganges for the sake of a single sentient being.

9. He is ever attentive to the mental activity of all sentient beings and the means to tame them.

10. His meditative stabilisation is equally placed upon the suchness of all phenomena.

11. Through wisdom he understands how the 84,000 heaps of doctrine are taught as appropriate antidotes to the delusive activity of beings to be tamed.

12. He does not fall away from the liberation wherein all obstructions have been thoroughly abandoned.

His virtuous activity is threefold:

13. His radiating light and the four modes of conduct etc., are physical virtuous activity.

14. Teaching appropriately to the inclinations of sentient beings is virtuous activity of speech.

15. His possessing love and great compassion is mental virtuous activity.

The three categories of his primordial wisdom are his direct knowledge of all phenomena of the past, present and future free from attachment and obscuration. These conclude the 18 unshared qualities of a Buddha.

He has boundless, magnificently brilliant and incomparable qualities, such as omniscience, directly seeing all phenomena comprising the aggregates, constituents and sources. The qualities of his compassion are such that by the force of his having perfected great compassion through repeated familiarity with it during his previous training on the path, there is no occasion when he does not generate sublime compassion for sentient beings tortured by sufferings. There are always sentient beings equal to the limits of space overwhelmed by many and various sufferings and it is impossible that he would ever be unaware of them; indeed, in observing them, his compassion always arises uninterruptedly,and therefore the welfare of wandering beings also arises perpetually.

His virtuous activity has two qualities; firstly, it occurs spontaneously. Although he makes no deliberate effort to perform the various miracles or the four modes of conduct of the form body of a Tathagata adorned with marks and signs, by seeing him the fortunate generate the mind of enlightenment, engage in the six perfections and so forth and thereby attain ultimate bliss. This is the way he manifests the spontaneous virtuous activity of his body.

The Buddha does not have the thought, "I will teach this," nevertheless he teaches infinite varieties of the doctrine suitable to the inclinations of those to be tamed. This is how he spontaneously manifests virtuous activity of speech.

While the Conquerors' great loving compassion does not have a motivating thought, they let fall showers of the holy doctrine that wandering beings may attain high status and definite goodness. This is how they manifest the spontaneous virtuous activity of mind.

There are no ordinary people who can perform the actions of body, speech and mind without effort, yet Bodhisattvas on the eighth ground have pacified the gross effort of motivation to teach the doctrine and so forth, and the welfare of others arises automatically. However, at that time the subtle thought motivating the actions of body, speech and mind has not been abandoned. The subtle conditions obstructing the spontaneous accomplishment of others' welfare are the so-called uncontaminated actions which are one of the 12 categories of obstructions to omniscience. They are the subtle motivating thoughts associated with the actions of body, mind and speech. Whenever they are overcome, the fulfilment of others' welfare will arise effortlessly and spontaneously.

Secondly, the Buddha's virtuous activity is unremitting. Formerly, while on the path he generated, dwelt in and progressively increased the exalted qualities included in the two collections and advanced serially through the 10 Bodhisattva grounds. That this excellent causal collection was achieved previously is the reason his virtuous activity is unremitting.

Moreover, the minds of sentient beings are not naturally associated with stains, but the Tathagata essence is obscured by delusions and their instincts. His great compassion is ever watchful to show the means which are a condition of overcoming such adventitious stains. Thus, it gives rise to the Buddha's spontaneous, unremitting virtuous activity.

Here I have briefly described the significance of ascertaining the presentation of the two levels of truth, how to advance upon the paths of the Mahayana and Hinayana dependent upon the three trainings and the practice of wisdom and method, which are contained in the three baskets of the words of the Able One (the Buddha), as well as the resultant Buddha's four bodies, his virtuous activity and so forth. It was not appropriate to give a presentation of the path in extensive detail here, so I have not attempted to do so.

# CHAPTER ELEVEN

## *An Introduction to the Different Traditions of the Buddhist Doctrine as They Existed in Tibet*

If the various schools upholding the noble tradition of the doctrine of our Teacher, the Lord Buddha, in our land of Tibet are explained briefly, it can be said that throughout the three regions of Tibet there was nowhere that the Buddha's Dharma did not prevail, indeed it flourished like the sun at its zenith. In addition, two periods may be distinguished, known as the early and later propagations of the doctrine.

The 33rd Tibetan King Choe-gyal Song-dzen-gam-po took control of the kingdom at the age of 13 and built the main temples in Lhasa and Tra-drag as well as many other temples such as Ta-dul and Ru-non. He sent his minister Tho-mi-sam-bho-ta to learn Sanskrit and writing, who then composed the Tibetan script modelled on that of India, and wrote eight works of grammar. He invited Acharya Kumara and Brahmin Shankara from India and Nepalese Acharya Shilamanju, who began the propagation of the doctrine and the translation of many of the Buddha's teachings of both sutra and tantra. Although there was neither conspicuous nor extensive study of the doctrine, the king himself gave instructions to many fortunate people, mostly concerning the teachings of the Great Compassionate One.

With the coming of the 37th king Tri-song-deu-dzen the holy doctrine was spread with great zeal. He invited the Abbot Shantarakshita from Zahor in Eastern India and the great Acharya Padmasambhava. This Abbot and Acharya and 108 renowned Indian scholars, such as Acharya Vimalamitra, Shantigarbha, Dharmakirti, Buddhaguhya, Kamalashila, Vibuddhasita, with the Tibetan translators, Vairochanna, Nyagjnana Kumara, Kawa Pel-dzeg, Chog-ro Lui-gyel-tsen, Shang-yeshe-de translated various sets of Buddha's sutra teachings concerning the Baskets of Discipline, Discourses and Knowledge, various sets of tantras and their principal textual commentaries, while establishing great centres of learning and practice.

The 41st King Tri-ral-pa-chen decreed that every monk should be supported by seven households and constructed thousands of temples. He would visualise the two assemblies of the peerless objects of devotion seated on the ends of the silk scarves which were tied to his hair and would worship them respectfully. Thus, he honoured the precious teaching of the Conqueror with limitless deeds. He invited many Indian scholars such as the Abbot Acharya Jinamitra, Surendrabodhi, Shilendrabodhi and Danashila, who, with the Tibetan Abbots Ratnarakshita, Dharmatashila, and the translators Jnanasena and Jayarakshita revised the translations done by scholars and translators during the reigns of previous kings, standardised them according to the texts of the Mahayana and Hinayana and clarified unintelligibility in the Tibetan language. Following the order of the king they divided the Extensive Mother (Perfection of Wisdom sutra) into 16 bundles. Likewise, most of the teachings translated previously were standardised according to the revised terminology and so forth, and the precious teaching of the Buddha was increasingly propagated throughout Tibet, the Land of Snow. This is known as the early propagation of the teaching.

The 42nd King Lang-darma eradicated Buddha's teaching. At that time Mar-sha-kya, Yo-ge-jung and Tsang-rab-sel, inheritors of the lineage of the great Abbot Shantarakshita, fled to Do-mey where they received full ordination from the great Lama Gong-pa-rab-sel. Thereafter, many monastic communities gradually arose. Subsequently, with the arrival of Dharmapala, Sadhupala and so on in upper Ngari and the coming of the great Kashmiri scholar Shakyashri further lineages of discipline came to Tibet and the ordained community was greatly expanded.

From that period onwards many Indian scholars and adepts came to Tibet and many Tibetan scholar translators went with great hardship to India and Nepal. Making offerings of gold they laid themselves at the feet of numerous scholars and adepts and received many teachings of both sutra and mantra which they translated and disseminated in Tibet. The lineage of scholars and yogis gradually developed from them and the precious teaching of the Able One which had degenerated was revived again. The teaching of Buddha, flourishing throughout Tibet, became like the brilliant sun, which is known as the later propagation of the teaching.

There are a number of different names for the various sects within the lineage of the doctrine in Tibet. For example Nying-ma-pa is a name given according to its era, Sha-kya-pa, Tag-lung-pa, Dri-gung-pa, Drug-pa and Gan-den-pa are names given according to their place of origin. Kar-ma Ka-gyu-pa, Bu-luk-pa are names given according to their teachers. Ka-dam-pa, Dzog-chen-pa, Chog-chen-pa, Shi-jay-pa are names given according to their precepts. These traditions of the Dharma can be grouped together as either the old or new systems.

How are the old and new systems different? The Mahayana teaching which flourished in Tibet included both sutra and tantra and whilst there is no divergence between the old and new presentations of sutra, the principal difference is found in their ways of propagating the Mahayana teaching of secret mantra. As explained above, the translations of secret mantra from the time of the early propagation until the arrival of Pandit Smirti are known as the early translations, and the holders of the lineages of practice and teaching are known as Nying-ma-pa. Translations from the period of the translator Rin-chen Zang-po are known as the new translations. The new translations of secret mantra were begun by Rin-chen Zang-po in 978 AD. Thereafter, Drog-mi, Ta-nag-go, Lo-drag Mar-pa and so forth gradually translated many sets of tantra into Tibetan and spread the teachings of the new translations of secret mantra extensively. These days, of the many schools of tenets which existed in Tibet the four most widespread are the Nying-ma school and of the new traditions the Ka-gyu-pa, Sa-kya-pa and Ge-lug-pa.

In 810 AD the great Acharya Padmasambhava came from Ugyen to Tibet, where he established eight great seats of learning centred around Sam-ye and translated many tantras and sadhanas. For his 25 foremost disciples and a gathering of the fortunate at such a place of learning he turned the wheel of the great secret vajra vehicle from which the secret mantra lineage of the Nying-ma tradition eventually arose.

Mar-ton Choe-kyi Lo-dro was born in 1012 and went to India

three times, where he studied at the feet of the great scholar Naropa, as well as Maitripa and many other gurus. He translated and explained many authoritative texts and the lineage coming from him through Je-tsun Mi-la-re-pa and the incomparable Dag-pa Hla-je is known as the Ka-gyu-pa tradition. Within the Ka-gyu-pa are four major and eight minor sub-sects such as the Kam-tsang-pa, Dri-gung-pa, Tag-lung-pa and Drug-pa.

Gon-kon-chog-Gyal-po, who was born in 1034 AD and studied at the feet of the translator Drog-mi received the lineage of "path and fruit" teachings derived from the Nalanda Abbot Shri Dharmapala, also known as Mahasiddha Virupa, and the great scholar Gayadhara. This is the lineage of the Sa-kya tradition maintained by the five Sa-kya Patriarchs.

In the year 1039 the great master of Vikramalashila, Dipamkara Shrijnana came to Tibet and spread the profound teachings of sutra and mantra. The lineage coming from his three disciples Ku-dron-tzon-dru Gyu-ong-drug, Ngog-Lo-tsa-wa Lo-dan Sherab and Drom-ton-pa Gyal-wai Jung-ne is known as the Ka-dam-pa.

The great Jam-gon Tsong-ka-pa, born 1357, was a holder of this lineage. By means of hearing, thinking and meditation he severed all doubts concerning the words of the Tathagata and the authoritative commentaries explaining their import, which were translated from the Indian language into Tibetan in the Land of Snow. He directed that the meaning of the profound teaching should be taught well and unmistakenly. His lineage, maintained by Gyal-tsab and Kay-drub and so on is known as the tradition of the Gan-den Mountain.

Some people might think that the Sa-kya, Ge-lug, Ka-gyu and Nying-ma traditions existing in Tibet were as entirely different and at variance in the presentation of basis, path and results as Buddhist and non-Buddhist schools. This is not the case, as may be clearly shown by reason. Nowadays, for example, aeroplanes can be seen flying in the sky; they differ externally in size, shape and colour, and specific internal mechanisms and model parts may vary somewhat according to the experience and ingenuity of each manufacturer. Yet, in fact, no matter how many types of aeroplane there are, no differences exist in as much as all fly in the sky dependent on the power of wind and fire. Thus, we recognise aeroplanes as being of one type. Similarly, the traditions of Buddhist doctrine in Tibet may differ slightly depending on the experience and skilful means in leading disciples on the path of the great and accomplished masters who were their original founders. Minor differences of terminology and custom exist, but essentially the ultimate achievement of these traditions of the Dharma is the same Buddhahood. As explained above, the stages of practice by which to accomplish that are none other than the combined practice of the three higher trainings, without breaching the four seals of the accepted view. There is no disagreement regarding the combined practice of sutra and mantra and in the final analysis all are one, having a common source.

Moreover, some have called the doctrine of Tibet "Lamaism" as if it were not the doctrine taught by Buddha. That is not so, because it was the Buddha who originally taught the sets of sutras and tantras which are the root source of all the Buddhist traditions in Tibet. In the middle period the great Indian scholars reaffirmed and taught the meaning of sutra and tantra based on the application of logic through the threefold correct analysis, while the great adepts and yogis put the profound instructions into practice and produced valid realisations within their mindstreams.

Finally, it is due to the kindness of the kings and ministers of Tibet, the Land of Snow, who were Bodhisattvas, and to the kindness of the past translators who, without a thought for wealth and resources, not even caring for hardships of body and life, with strenuous efforts went to India and Nepal like an unstoppable flow of water and, having made threefold requests to the indisputably renowned scholars and adepts, received the teachings, that those very teachings were translated into Tibetan and taken as the root and basis for engaging in the three practices of hearing, thinking and meditating. There is nothing else invented by Tibetan lamas which contradicts this doctrine. For instance, should the slightest need arise to clarify doubts about the salient points of the doctrine or to trace their source, any Tibetan Buddhist, whoever he or she may be, would refer either to the Buddha's teaching or to the works of the Indian scholars and adepts.

# Part Two

# Generating a Good Heart

# GENERATING A GOOD HEART

If you are a religious person you must put the Dharma into actual practice, not leaving it merely as words. Essentially this practice should help you tame your mind and give practical evidence of doing so. Those of us who work ought to make our contributions to the common cause as we have undertaken to do.

As I have said before, if when it comes to being of help to others we become holier-than-thou but do nothing, yet where our own interests are concerned our actions follow our words—then something is wrong. We may say, 'I take refuge in the Buddha, Dharma and Sangha' and adopt a sanctimonious manner, a devout expression, but in practice it is very difficult for us to sacrifice even such a dry thing as our name and reputation, not to mention giving up our lives for the sake of others. As we can clearly see from our own experience, we dare not give up even small things and cannot bear the slightest loss, because basically we are selfish. Take the example of some task for the common good—our pretentious talk about it resounds like a false clap of thunder, but in fact when it comes to putting it into action we have nothing to offer. We think of accomplishing our own ends by deceiving or flattering others, by wheedling behaviour and cunning or by whatsoever other means we can think of. Thus, the common cause is never fulfilled.

So, all of us should try not to be like this, for if we follow a Dharma practice we should not idly put on a pious face when it comes to helping others, but should be realistic about it in thought and deed. Though we may not be in a position to give up our own interests, we should be modest and considerate in accomplishing them. As we are all responsible for the common good we should not merely adopt a sanctimonious expression when something needs to be done, but should sincerely put all our efforts into fulfilling it. As I said before, it is difficult to sacrifice our own aims, but although each of us individually needs to obtain our own livelihood, if the means of doing so makes an honest contribution to the common good, so much the better.

We should regularly turn our minds within and investigate whether we are sincere or not, irrespective of what others may think. From our own point of view we should principally rely on the two powers (mindfulness and introspection) and while we should be careful to create no cause for regret or embarrassment, we should obviously be discreet and well-mannered whether we are in public or at home. If we act in this way, happiness will naturally be ours.

It is never good to misbehave until someone warns us. In this world of many nations with their different cultures and standards, though it functions smoothly in some ways, yet murder, rape, robbery and deceit are committed merely to fulfil the individual's unlawful aims. This is quite clear and it is therefore of utmost importance that we human beings should behave with consideration and self-restraint, whether there is someone to warn us or not, particularly we Tibetans who have lost our homeland and are scattered in many alien countries.

If we behave modestly and in accordance with the law of cause and effect, it is certain that in the short term we will enjoy mental peace and ultimately, when we are at the brink of death, we will be able to go peacefully; while at the same time society will also benefit. The point here is that it is important that we Tibetans should behave modestly according to the law of the land and if we do the results will be good.

Over and above that, if we work hard to accumulate merit we will derive benefit in proportion to our effort. If we are successful in accumulating merit it makes a corresponding difference to our ability to accomplish our work; so gathering merit is important. The best way of doing so, as I have told you before, is to generate a good heart—there is nothing better than this. If the Buddhas and Bodhisattvas were to meet and discuss the best way of gaining merit, they would find nothing better than this. Therefore, although it may be difficult for us to generate the actual mind of enlightenment and the two-fold aspiration (to benefit self and others), if we can even simulate doing so the merit acquired will be great.

As all of us, even ants, desire happiness and do not wish for suffering, we all have an equal right to acquire happiness and eliminate suffering, as well as ultimately to be freed from all sufferings and endowed with happiness. Taking this as the basic point, no matter how important we think we are, we must think of ourselves as equal to an ant, compared to the infinity of other beings throughout the expanse of space.

While no one speaks of democracy as a Bodhisattva ideal, in reality, if the minority were to make sacrifices for the sake of the majority, that would indeed be something appropriate and worthwhile. Take for example an animal with a kind heart: it is plain to see that as long as he does not harm his fellows, others gather around him, are happy with him and like him. Similarly, if a man is less selfish and thinks of others as much as he can, then people in general will regard him as devoted to the welfare of others, will praise him, refer to him as a good man and will love and respect him. This is an obvious example from our own lives. However, we normally strive to acquire happiness for ourselves and to eliminate our own sufferings, but if we were to take the same responsibility for others as we do for ourselves, we would be pricelessly valuable and everyone would recognise us as someone worthy of respect. India's Mahatma Gandhi is such an example; because he sacrificed himself for others, people naturally loved him.

What Mahayana Buddhism teaches is this: from the very core of our heart we should sacrifice our life, possessions, and merit for the sake of other sentient beings as we find in *A Guide to the Bodhisattva's Way of Life*:

> When both myself and others
> Are similar in that we wish to be happy
> What is so special about me?
> Why do I strive for my happiness alone?
> And when both myself and others
> Are similar in that we do not wish to suffer
> What is so special about me?
> Why do I protect myself and not others?

It is said that because our own and others' desire for happiness is the same from all angles, there is no reason whatsoever to exert ourselves in seeking our own happiness alone without thinking of others, nor should we exert ourselves to eliminate only our own suffering when others' wish to be free from suffering is equal to our own. It is further said:

'If I give this away, what shall I use for myself?'
Such selfish thinking is the way of ghosts.
'If I enjoy this, what shall I have left to give?'
Such altruistic thinking is a quality of gods.

So, to think, 'If I give this away to others, what shall I use for myself?' is described as a devilish and inferior way of thinking, while the opposite thought, 'If I enjoy this, what shall I have left for others?' is described as a divine, superior thought, which should be cultivated. If we exploit others for our own ends, such a shameless attitude may result in a bad rebirth or our becoming the servant of others, whereas to give of ourself for the sake of others may result in the state of liberation and omniscience. In short:

All the drawbacks of this world
Derive from a desire for one's own happiness,
And all the joys of this world
Derive from a desire for the happiness of others.
What more need be said?
Ordinary beings work for their own benefit,
The Buddhas work for the benefit of others.
Just look at the difference between them.

Now, the one we refer to as Lord Buddha, whom we worship and revere today, was once himself the same as us. When he was a trainee on the path, he too was filled with poisonous delusions. Now he is free of all faults and has perfected all qualities, so why are we still under the sway of delusions, roaming here and there in cyclic existence—what is the cause? What is the difference? It is because Buddha worked only for the welfare of others and never thought of his own benefit. That is how he freed himself of all faults and became enlightened.

Although we all desire happiness and do not want suffering, we are still under the sway of the three root delusions and are unable to help either ourself or anyone else. This pathetic situation is the unfortunate result of our selfish outlook and therefore all of us should endeavour to generate a good heart. Bringing about the welfare of others is absolutely flawless, from start to finish, temporarily and permanently, being neither flattering nor backbiting. Whoever we are, if we are able to cultivate such a good heart, we will not only be flawless ourselves, but we will receive inconceivable benefits; so should we not generate such a noble thought? If we are able to do so, not only will each of us enjoy happiness, even in this life, but those around us will enjoy peace and quiet too.

When we speak of sentient beings equal to the extent of space, we should not just think of sentient beings in general, but should think specifically of our parents, relatives and neighbours, those we usually associate with, as well as those for whom we feel attachment, anger or resentment. Thus, including those close to us as human beings, living creatures should be the principal object when we think of sentient beings equal to space. If we are able to cultivate a good heart in this way, we will be happy ourselves and our fellows will also enjoy leisure, peace and happiness. If we lack a rich diet and have only simple food to eat, we will be able to eat it with relish. When we experience difficulties we will be confident enough to rely on others and seek their help. However, if on the contrary we are selfish and jealous of others, if we compete with them, deceive them and think only of harming them, then even when we share the same house with them we will live in an atmosphere of mutual suspicion and distrust. We cannot expect to find any real peace or leisure in such a home or neighbourhood, nor even any personal security.

If we were to be good-hearted, courteous and always giving priority to others' welfare, looking after our own secondly, it would obviously be beneficial to ourself and society at large, both temporarily and ultimately. Such behaviour would be a source of happiness and a cause for gathering merit as well as for minimising negativity in the years that remain of the short span of our life, not to speak of it being a cause for attaining high states of birth, liberation and ultimately omniscience, in future lives. If on the contrary, we only cultivate a selfish outlook, then even in the short term we are unable to gain happiness, let alone the state of omniscience. This has been clearly stated in *A Guide to the Bodhisattva's Way of Life:*

> If I do not actually exchange my happiness
> For the sufferings of others,
> I shall not attain the state of Buddhahood
> And even in cyclic existence shall have no joy.

If we do not have an urge to exchange our own happiness for

the suffering of others, there is no chance of our attaining Buddha-hood, nor even of gaining happiness in this life—this is obvious.

Even for a lama, a guru, a monk or a nun, those who have a good heart naturally become the object of others' respect, whereas those with a selfish motive may receive respect to their faces, but behind their backs people will ask, 'What use is his being a lama, guru etc?' Since they are free to speak they will do so, which may not be undeserved. Similarly, when a leader is strongly motivated by selfishness, although people may show respect and shower praises on him in his presence, later on if he meets with problems they will rejoice, which is natural.

So all of us should try our best to cultivate a good heart towards others and give up selfish motives. In this the Dharma accords with the ways of the world; it brings happiness to self and others both temporarily and ultimately, andnothing is superior to this. If we were to bow down before the Buddha himself, he would only give the same advice as can be seen clearly in the collection of his teachings.

The essential point of the Mahayana teaching is to help others, while the essential point of the Hinayana teaching is not to harm others. These two phrases 'help others if possible' and 'if not, do not harm them' between them condense the meaning of all the 84,000 heaps of Buddha's teaching.

If we believe in religious teachings, this is the lifetime when we have found this precious human birth and have met with Buddha's teaching, which is difficult to do, and moreover we have met with the Mahayana and within it the combination of the teachings of sutra and tantra. Indeed, the teachings of all the four religious traditions in Tibet have the quality of being a union of sutra and tantra, enabling us to attain enlightenment in a single lifetime.

At present, when you have met with qualified masters, even though you may not be able to actualise all the Mahayana teach-ings, it is important that from now onwards you try to make a good start by planting positive seeds so you may be able to gain enlight-enment in future lives. You should resolve to gain enlightenment for sentient beings throughout space, who all equally desire happi-ness and do not want suffering, and should work for their welfare and benefit to the best of your ability.

However, merely generating a good heart is not sufficient

without the further conditions necessary to benefit others; therefore you should seek correct practical guidance from qualified masters in order to reach that ultimate state capable of accomplishing the welfare of others, because if you yourself lack the knowledge of such means you will be unable to help them. If you are to be in a position to lead others through your own experience, you must actualise correct paths of realisation within yourself and familiarise yourself with them by putting them into practice.

Who is able to work incessantly for the welfare of all sentient beings throughout space, irrespective of time or class of being? It is only a fully accomplished Buddha. In brief, to be capable of completely fulfilling the wishes of all sentient beings is a quality exclusive to Buddhas, so it is important to generate a good heart, aspiring to generate the noble mind of enlightenment for the sake of others. As a prerequisite for generating this good heart we should pray, "May all the virtues that I have accumulated through body, speech and mind become a cause for doing this." If we cultivate a good heart in this way, the benefit will be immeasurable, as has been taught in *A Guide to the Bodhisattva's Way of Life*.

Now the way to make prayers for generating this immeasurably good heart is like this; firstly, we should accumulate merits through performing the seven limb practice. Although confession is included there, to strengthen our confession practice it is good to follow the example of past holy masters by reciting the Confession Sutra while prostrating—this is really very good. As it says in *A Guide to the Bodhisattva's Way of Life*:

> All the Buddhas and Bodhisattvas have unobstructed
> vision at all times.

So we should think that we are in their ever-watchful presence and that the 35 Buddhas of Confession are actually in the space before us. You can think that I am here leading the ceremony. Then recite the Confession Sutra very slowly while reflecting on what it means. Develop a strong sense of regret for all the heaps of misdeeds that you and all sentient beings have accumulated through the activities of body, speech and mind, which have obstructed the generation of this good heart, and resolve not to commit them again even at the cost of your life. While doing this, make prostrations.

Now to begin the actual practice of generating the awakening mind, we can recite this prayer:

I go for refuge until enlightenment
To the Buddha, Dharma and supreme community.
By the virtue of my deeds such as giving
May I attain Buddhahood in order to benefit wander-
     ing beings.

The first two lines concern taking refuge in the Buddha, Dharma and Sangha. It is the Buddha who has accomplished all qualities and exhausted all faults. He is our teacher, showing us what to abandon and what to adopt. The Dharma of cessation and path refer to the gradual exhaustion of all faults and the means to gain all qualities respectively, while those Bodhisattvas on or above the first ground who possess these two, the cessation and path of Mahayana, in their mindstreams are the Supreme Community whom we take as our example and upon whom we can rely as trustworthy friends. So while saying, "I go for refuge, etc", take refuge in the Buddha, Dharma and Sangha from the depth of your heart.

When you say the next two lines make a strong resolution, "Here and now I have met with the Mahayana teaching, which is a union of sutra and tantra, because I have gathered roots of virtue in many past lives. Now I shall generate the precious mind of enlightenment which cherishes others before self and I will train according to it and achieve unsurpassable enlightenment. And from now onwards, whatever my deeds of body, speech and mind may be, I dedicate them to all sentient beings."

In short, as holy Nagarjuna has said:

Always make yourself available
For the welfare of sentient beings,
Just as earth, water, fire, wind, medicine
And forests (are available to all).

and:

May I be as dear to sentient beings as their
Own life and may they be very dear to me.
May their misdeeds bear fruit for me,

And all my virtues ripen for them.
As long as there are sentient beings
Who have not found liberation,
May I remain (in the world) for their sake
Even though I have attained enlightenment.

Shantideva's *A Guide to the Bodhisattva's Way of Life* says:

Just like space
And the great elements such as earth
May I always support the life
Of all the boundless creatures.

and:

For as long as space endures
And for as long as living beings remain,
Until then may I too abide
To dispel the misery of the world.

You should think, "May I become like the Mahasattva Avalokiteshvara, who shows great courage and spares no effort in working for the welfare of sentient beings as long as space endures," and resolve that you too will behave in this way.

Now, with a wish not to waste all the roots of virtue we have accumulated until today, we should make strong prayers and wishes that these may be a cause for attaining the state of supreme enlightenment. It is by means of such strong prayers that we generate a good heart.

Now let us say the seven limb prayer. While visualising the Buddhas and Bodhisattvas of the 10 directions in the space in front of you repeat the verse, 'I go for refuge to the Buddha, Dharma and Supreme Community etc,' after me, who you may think of as their agent.

Today we have generated a good heart according to the aspirational method on the basis of the two collections (of merit and insight) that we have gathered previously. It is taught in *A Guide to the Bodhisattva's Way of Life* that this has inconceivable benefits and, as I have already said, just as we have generated a good heart today, so we should be kind-hearted in our daily life. If we are unable to help others, at least we should not harm them—

we should take this precept as the essential motive for our lives and avoid breaking it.

*A Guide to the Bodhisattva's Way of Life* says:

> Today my life has (borne) fruit.
> Having obtained this good human existence
> I have been born in the family of Buddha
> And now am one of Buddha's sons.
> Thus whatever actions I do from now on
> Must be in accord with the family.
> Never shall I disgrace or pollute
> This noble and unsullied lineage.

It is very fortunate that at this time we have generated this good heart which is so rarely found. We have made our lives fruitful, because today we have been born into the family of Buddhas through generating a good heart in accordance with the Buddha's teachings, and therefore we must work hard to maintain it.

Now how do we carry out this practice? Just as the Buddhas and their sons think only of other sentient beings and do only what is of benefit to them, so we too must try to follow this in thought and deed and abide by it.

We will make the dedication as Manjushri, Samantabhadra and Avalokiteshvara have done so, with this in mind, let us recite these prayers together.

> Just as the hero Manjushri has understood
> And likewise Samantabhadra too,
> I dedicate these virtues
> That I may follow their ways.
> Just as all the Buddhas of the three times
> Make dedication to that which is well-praised
> So do I dedicate all my virtues
> That I too may train in goodness.

# GLOSSARY

Terms are followed in brackets by the Tibetan and then the Sanskrit equivalent where appropriate.

*aggregates (phung po—skandha)* all impermanent phenomena belonging to either a sentient being's personal continuum or the external world can be divided into the five aggregates, or literally, heaps; the aggregates are mental and physical, because the first, form, is physical while the remaining four are mental aggregates.

*Asanga (c. 400 AD)* an Indian Buddhist master who was a major proponent of Mahayana Buddhism, he received many important teachings including those of the method lineage from Arya Maitreya.

*baskets, three (sde snod gsum—tripitaka)* the general classification of the Buddha's actual teachings into the Baskets of Discipline, Discourses and Knowledge; when these teachings were eventually written down the looseleaf books were bound together and stored in baskets.

*Bodhisattva (byang chub sems pa)* one who has actualised an aspiration to attain enlightenment for the sake of all beings and who has embarked on the path to fulfil that goal.

*Bodhisattva ground (byang chub sems pa'i sa—Bodhisattvabhumi)* once a Bodhisattva has achieved insight into reality on the path of seeing he attains the first ground or level; there are 10 grounds of development in his progress to complete enlightenment.

*boundless action (mtsams med kyi las—anutariyani—karma)* an action of such negative power that its unwholesome consequences have no limit; five such actions are commonly cited—i. killing one's father, ii. killing one's mother, iii. killing a Foe Destroyer, iv. drawing blood from a Buddha, v. causing a schism in the spiritual community.

*Buddha (sangs rgyas)* historically Shakyamuni, the Sage of Shakyas, founder of the tradition now known as Buddhism; one who has achieved all qualities and eradicated all faults; a fully evolved mind.

*Buddha-field (sangs rgyas kyi zhing—Buddhakshetra)* spiritual environment produced as a result of the blessings of a fully enlightened being and the pure vision of his close disciples; it has no fixed spatial location.

*calm abiding (zhi gnas—shamatha)* means of pacifying the mind so it is undistracted by external objects and able to dwell single-pointedly on the mental objects of meditation; a practice common to Buddhism and other Indian religions.

*Chandragomin (c. 700 AD)* a great scholar at Nalanda University, India, particularly renowned for his skill in poetic composition.

*Chandrakirti (c. 700 AD)* a great exponent of both the perfection and tantric vehicles of the Mahayana; he is specially renowned for clarifying the thought of Nagarjuna and establishing the school of Prasangika-Madhyamika.

*Confession Sutra (ltungs bshags—trikandhasutra)* a sutra including the names of 35 Buddhas and a declaration of moral downfalls, commonly recited as a prayer of confession.

*Conqueror (rgyal ba—Jina)* an epithet of Buddha.

*cyclic existence ('khor ba—samsara)* Buddhist conception of beings' existence as a beginningless cycle of births propelled by actions and delusions and characterised by suffering, which will only cease when liberation is attained.

*delusion (nyon mongs—klesha)* mental factors which disturb the mind and thereby give rise to unwholesome actions whose result is suffering; the three root delusions are desire, hatred and ignorance.

*Desire Realm ('dod khams—kamadhatu)* realm of sentient beings whose minds are preoccupied by desire for sensual objects; within it are all categories of sentient beings except gods of the form and formless realms.

*desire delusions ('dod nyon—kamaklesha)* delusions specific to the beings of the desire realm.

*dependent-arising (rten 'brel/rten 'byung—pratitya samutpada)* formulation of the idea of emptiness of inherent existence in terms of conventional phenomena; lacking inherent existence all phenomena are dependent on something else e.g. causes and conditions, moments, parts, directions etc.

*Dharma (chos)* a term with many connotations, here generally meaning the teaching of the Buddha and hence the Dharma Jewel or Refuge; the Sanskrit term has been used here where there is a sense of practice and realisation of the teaching; where only what was taught is referred to, it has been rendered as doctrine.

*elements, four (khams bzhi—caturthadhatu)* earth, water, fire and air and the qualities they represent, i.e. solidity, liquidity, heat and motility.

*Foe Destroyer (dgra bcom pa—Arhat)* one who has attained peace or liberation by destroying his or her delusions, which are characterised as the foe because they give rise to suffering.

*Forder (mu steg pa—Tirthika)* an Indian religious sect derived, according to some, from the Samkhya philosophical school; they assert a permanent, partless, independent self.

*Form realm (gzugs khams—rupadhatu)* a realm where the mind is principally occupied in meditation on pure form; beings abiding there have a form and are known as form gods.

*Formless realm (gzugs med khams—arupadhatu)* a realm where the mind is engaged in one of the four formless absorptions; beings abiding there lack form and are known as formless gods.

*four modes of conduct (spyod pa rnam bzhi—caturvidha cara)* walking, standing, sitting and reclining.

*Great Compassionate One (thugs rje chen po—Mahakarunikaya)* epithet of Avalokiteshvara, the Bodhisattva embodying compassion.

*guru (bla ma)* literally 'one heavy with qualities', spiritual master; personal religious teacher.

*Hearer (nyan thos—Shravaka)* originally a direct disciple of Buddha, who had actually heard his teachings and then practised and proclaimed them; now commonly refers to a Hinayanist who strives for his or her own liberation and relies on a teacher during his or her training.

*Hedonist (rgyang 'phen pa—Charavaka)* proponents of non-Buddhist tenets who assert the non-existence of past and future lives and thus deny a basis for observing ethics.

*Heterodox (phyi rol pa—bahihra)* literally 'outsider', non-Buddhists in general, although historically it refers to the teachers and doctrines of the six ancient Indian schools of thought.

*Highest Pure Land ('og min—Akanishta)* the highest heaven of the form realm where a Bodhisattva of the 10th ground attains enlightenment in the form of the complete enjoyment body.

*Hinayana (theg dman)* literally `the lessor vehicle'; the path followed by Hearers and Solitary Realisers leading to personal liberation from cyclic existence alone.

*isolate (ldog pa—apeksha)* opposite of the negative; a logical formulation by which to distinguish phenomena which are the same entity; for example, table and product are the same entity because table is a product; however, because non-table (eg. cup) and non-product (eg. space) are different, it is said that their opposites of the negatives, i.e. non-non-table and non-non-product, are different.

*Jewels, Three (dkon mchog gsum—Triratna)* the three objects of refuge from the perils of cyclic existence, the Buddha, Dharma and Sangha or Spiritual Community, who are likened to the physician, the medicine or treatment and the nurses respectively.

*Joyous Land (dga'lden—Tushita)* at the peak of the six heavens of the desire realm, this is the land from which Buddha Shakyamuni descended to take the birth in which he would reveal enlightenment, and similarly it is where the future Buddha Maitreya now abides.

*liberation (thar pa—moksha)* freedom from the sufferings of cyclic existence, gained by overcoming the obstructions to liberation.

*Mahasattva Avalokiteshvara (sems pa chen po spyan ras gzigs)* the great Bodhisattva embodying compassion, with whom the Tibetans have a special bond.

*Mahayana (theg chen)* the great vehicle; the vehicle of Bodhisattvas leading to the great liberation of Buddhahood, which is sought not for individual peace alone, but to be able to benefit all beings.

*Maitreya (byams pa)* literally `loving-kindness'; the name of the future Buddha who will be fifth of the thousand Buddhas to appear in this fortunate age.

*Manjushri ('jam dpal dbyangs)* the youthful Bodhisattva embodying wisdom.

*meditative stabilisation (ting nge 'dzin—samadhi)* concentration; the ability of the mind to abide on a specific object of cognition for a period of time, which is achieved by practice of meditation.

*naga (klu)* beings classified as animals believed to live under the earth, having influence over ponds, streams, water-sources and soil fertility; they can be Dharma protectors and are depicted as half-human, half-serpent.

*Nagarjuna (c. 150 AD)* prophesied by the Buddha, he was the crucial disseminator of the Mahayana, formulator of the profound Middle Way (Madhyamika) philosophy, having reclaimed the Perfection of Wisdom sutras from the safe-keeping of the nagas.

*Noble Truths, Four ('phags pa'i bden pa bzhi—catuharyasathani)* commonly accepted name for the Buddha's first teaching; the four truths concern suffering, the origins of suffering, their cessation and the path; they are noble because they are realised by noble or superior beings.

*perfection vehicle (pha rol tu phyin pa'i theg pa—paramitayana)* one of the divisions of the Mahayana, the vehicle of Bodhisattvas following the practice of the six perfections—giving, ethics, patience, effort, meditation and wisdom; such practice will yield enlightenment in three countless aeons.

*Prasangika Madhyamika (thal 'gyur pa)* a Madhyamika who does not assert that phenomena exist by way of their own character even conventionally; the highest school of tenets founded by Chandrakirti on the basis of Nagarjuna's exposition of Madhyamika thought.

*sadhana (sgrub thabs)* method of actualisation; tantric meditation aimed at actualisation of reality by means of visualisation accompanied by rituals and recitations related to a certain deity.

*Samantabhadra (kun tu bzang po)* one of the eight Bodhisattvas regarded as close spiritual sons of Buddha Shakyamuni; Samantabhadra is noted for his remarkable practice of making extensive offerings.

*Sangha (dge'dun)* the spiritual community, generally of monks and nuns; conventionally the Sangha Refuge is an assembly of four or more monks, but any practitioner who has gained insight into emptiness and attained the rank of superior is himself or herself the ultimate Sangha Refuge.

*secret mantra (gsang snags—guhya mantra)* literally `secret mind protector'; often a series of syllables to be recited, visualised etc, thereby providing protection to the mind; used as a synonym for the tantric path and practice of the vajra vehicle.

*seven limb practice/prayer (yan lag bdun)* a practice whose seven limbs include prayers of prostration or homage, offering, confession, rejoicing at virtue, requesting the gurus to teach and to live long and dedication of merit, which is performed as a basic preliminary practice.

*Shantarakshita (c. 750 AD)* a proponent of Sautrantika Madhyamika who was an important teacher in India prior to being invited to Tibet, where he played a considerable role, along with Padmasambhava, in establishing the practice of Buddhism.

*Shantideva (c. 100 AD)* a monk at Nalanda Monastic University who followed the Prasangika tradition of Chandrakirti; his *Compendium of Training* and *Guide to the Bodhisattva's Way of Life* are two of the most popular works in all Mahayana literature.

*Solitary Realiser (rang sangs—Pratyekabuddha)* a practitioner of the Hinayana who has realised suchness and who in his or her last lifetime practises alone without depending on a teacher.

*special insight (lhag mthong—vipashyana)* based on the attainment of calm abiding, special insight is the result of the union of analytical and concentrated meditation on emptiness.

*superimposition (sgro'dogs—samaropita)* overestimation; exaggerating a phenomenon's mode of existence; attributing more qualities to a phenomenon than it has.

*Superior (`phags pa—Aryan)* beings who have risen above the level of common beings through realising emptiness directly on the path of seeing.

*Sutra (mdo)* words spoken by the Buddha, whether a discourse or a few words or phrases; within the Mahayana the sutra path refers to the perfection vehicle as distinct from the tantric vehicle.

*Svetaketu (dam pa tog dkar po)* immediately prior to the birth in which he became Shakyamuni, he was Svetaketa, regent of the Joyous Land.

*Tantra (rgyud)* category of Buddha's teachings concerning the secret mantra, vajra vehicle.

*Tathagata (bde bzhin bshegs pa)* literally `one thus gone'; an epithet for the Buddha.

*three times (dus gsum—trikala)* past, present and future.

*Vasubandhu (c. 400 AD)* brother of Asanga, who converted him from being a staunch Hinayanist to being a Mahayanist; particularly noted for his work *Treasury of Knowledge (Abhidharmakosha)*.

*wandering being ('gro ba—gotra)* literally `traveller, migrator'; a being who wanders from life to life within cyclic existence.

*Yogi (rnal 'byor pa)* an advanced practitioner of meditation.

# BIBLIOGRAPHY

**Sutras and Tantras**

*The King of Meditative Stabilisation Sutra*
Samadhiraja sutra
Ting nge 'dzin rgyal po'i mdo
P 795 vol. 31-2

*The Meeting of Father and Son Sutra*
Pitaputrasamagama sutra
Yab dang sras mjal ba'i mdo
P 760 16 Vol. 23

*Vajrapanjara Tantra*
Dakinivajrapanjaramahatantrajakalpa
mKha' 'gro ma rdo rje gur zhes bya ba'i rgyud
·P II Vol. II

**Sanskrit Treatises in Tibetan Translation**

Asanga (Thogs med)
*Compendium of Knowledge*
Abhidharmasamuchchaya
mNgon pa Kun btus
P 5550 Vol. 112

Chandrakirti (Zla ba grags pa)
*70 Verses on the Three Refuges*
Trisharanasaptati
gsum la skyabs su 'gro ba bdun cu pa
P 53666 Vol. 103

*Supplement to (Nagarjuna's) `Treatise on the Middle Way'*
Madhyamakavatara
dbu ma la 'jug pa
P 5261 Vol. 98, P 5262 Vol. 98

Maitreya (Byams pa)
*Discrimination of the Middle Way and the Extremes*
Madhyantavibhanga
dbus dang mtha 'a rnam par 'byed pa
P 5522 Vol. 108

*Ornament for Clear Realisations*
Abhisamayalamkara
mNgon par rtogs pa'i rgyan
P 5184 Vol. 88

*Ornament for the Mahayana Sutras*
Mahayanasutralamkarakarika
Theg pa chen po'i mod sde'i rgyan gyi tshig le'ur byas pa
P 5521 Vol. 108

Nagarjuna (kLu sgrub)
*Friendly Letter*
bShes pa'i springs yig
P 5682 Vol. 129

*Fundamental Treatise on the Middle Way, called Wisdom*
Prajnanamula madhyamaka karika
dbu ma rtsa ba'i tshig le'ur byas pa shes rab cas bya ba
P 5224 Vol. 95

Shantarakshita (Zhi ba 'tsho)
*Ornament for the Middle Way*
Madhyamakalamkara
dbu ma'i rgyan gyi tshig le'ur byas pa
P 5284 Vol. 10

Shantideva (Zhi ba lha)
*A Guide to the Bodhisattva's Way of Life*
Bodhisattvacharyavatara
Byang chub sems dpa'i spyod pa la 'jug pa
P 5272 Vol.99

Tripitakamala (sDe snod gsum phreng)
*Lamp for the Three Modes*
Mayatrayapradipa
Tsul gsum gyi sgron ma
P 4530 Vol. 81

Vasubandhu (dByig gnyen)
   *Treasury of Knowledge*
      Abhidharmakoshakarika
      Chos mngon pa'i mdzod ki bshad pa
      P 5591 Vol. 115

## Other Works:

Batchelor, Stephen. *Alone with Others,* New York: Grove Press, 1983.
—— *Echoes of Voidness,* London: Wisdom, 1983
—— *A Guide to the Bodhisattva's Way of Life,* Dharamsala: LTWA, 1979.

Beresford, Brian. *Mahayana Purification,* Dharamsala: LTWA, 1980.

Berzin, Alex tr. & ed. *Anthology of Well-spoken Advice,* Dharamsala: LTWA, 1982.

Conze, Edward tr. *The Perfection of Wisdom in Eight Thousand Lines and its Verse Summary.* Bolinas: Four Seasons Foundation, 1973.

Dhargyey, Geshey Ngawang. *Tibetan Tradition of Mental Development,* Dharamsala: LTWA, 1974.

Hopkins, Jeffrey. tr. *Compassion in Tibetan Buddhism,* London: Rider, 1980.
—— *Meditation on Emptiness.* London: Wisdom, 1983.
—— tr. *Precious Garland and Song of Four Mindfulnesses,* London: George Allen and Unwin, 1975.

Sopa, Geshe Lhundup, and Hopkins, Jeffrey. *Practice and Theory of Tibetan Buddhism.* London: Rider, 1976.

Sakya Dragpa Gyaltsen. *Chandragomin's Twenty Verses on the Bodhisattva Vow and its Commentary.* tr. Mark Tatz. Dharamsala: LTWA, 1982.

Tharchin, Geshe Lobsang and Engle, Artemus B. *Nagarjuna's Letter,* Dharamsala: LTWA, 1977.

Zehle, Leah, ed. *Meditative States in Tibetan Buddhism,* London: Wisdom, 1983.